The Uncensored Guide to Maine

The Uncensored Guide to Maine

By Mark Melnicove
& Kendall Merriam

LANCE TAPLEY, PUBLISHER

Front cover photograph by C. Richard Coburn.

Back cover photographs by Sheila Garrett (left) and Mark Melnicove (right).

Title page cartoon by Peter Farrow.

Printed in the United States of America.

Library of Congress Cataloging in Publication Data

Melnicove, Mark.
    The uncensored guide to Maine.

    1. Maine--Description and travel--1981-   --Guide-
books. 2. Maine--Anecdotes, facetiae, satire, etc.
I. Merriam, Kendall. II. Title.
F17.3.M45 1984   917.41'0443   84-12759
ISBN 0-912769-02-5

   THIRD PRINTING

Dedicated to the last Ice Age,

which had the good grace to melt and uncover the tale you are about to read

Publisher's Disclaimer

Don't get me wrong. I like seagulls, clamshell ashtrays, L.L. Bean's, and fir balsam pillows as much as anybody. I didn't want to make fun of Maine. I know better than to take on a hundred years of sentimentality laid on so thick the state slips from your grasp like a harbor pollock. But look, I'm only *helping*, mind you. I'm only the publisher. The authors are the people to blame. They wrote this. Everybody knows writers are crazy. One of them is from away, so what does he know? The other was born in Rockland, and that's even worse! They're poor, ungrateful *writers*, for God's sake, which means they can't even keep a nine to five job — mere barnacles on our stately ship. I'm sure somebody will scrape 'em out of state after this book appears. Probably a reviewer from *Down East*. Good riddance. If they go far enough away I won't have to pay them royalties.

Royalties. Brings up the matter of money. Yes, it was money, that Yankee failing, that drove me to it. Yes, selling the state for $9.95. A Judas. Yes, just like a thousand other bloodsuckers...But there is a difference: This is the *real* Maine, the authentic item, worn-out long johns and all. And, who knows? Maybe some fresh air and sunshine will be good for our musty laundry. As much as the authors are scornful of reformers, maybe there's some small socially redeeming quality here.

I realized I had to publish this book after I had a dream in which one of my salt-sprayed ancestors spoke to me. He was the ship captain (one of seven brothers who were ship captains) who, after his wife died aboard his ship off the coast of Panama, pickled her in a barrel until she could be properly buried in Brooksville. Stroking his long beard, and speaking in a stern voice, he declared: "Son, the Maine way is 'Give 'em hell!' "

Ayuh.

LANCE TAPLEY

THE STATE OF MAINE SONG

Grand State of Maine,
Every Mainer would proudly sing
This song to you,
Except no one knows the words
To it, not even
The Governor has a clue.

Should schoolteachers unkind
Send schoolchildren to roam
To the State Library, to look up
The words of this song, perhaps
The scent of fragrant pines
And the tang of the salty sea
Will distract them enough
To forget about singing of thee.

Oh, Pine Tree State,
Your woods, fields and hills,
Your lakes, streams and rock-bound coast
Will ever fill our hearts with thrills,
And tho' we try hard to remember
The words to this song
Our efforts will be in vain,
Cause you don't care anyway,
Do you, Maine?

Contents

History of Maine, Revised

MAINE BEGINS WITH A BANG

It happened twenty billion years ago: KABOOM! And Maine (along with the rest of the Universe) was born. This explosion, the largest in Maine's history, is called The Big Bang. According to guidebooks of the time, there was no Mount Katahdin to climb and no Penobscot Bay to sail. The only thing to do, we are told, was sit back and try to enjoy the heat. This wasn't easy, however, as the average temperature was about a trillion degrees.

THE ICE AGE COMETH

It took a long time for things to cool off after The Big Bang, about 19,998,000,000 years. Finally, Mainers saw their first snow and ice. Unfortunately the animals, who were the only Mainers then, had grown used to the heat, had nothing to wear, and many died of exposure.

MAINERS BEGIN EATING THE SCENERY

About thirteen thousand years ago, things warmed up enough to allow caribou, mastodons, wooly mammoths, giant beavers and other animals to come live in Maine. They ate off the flourishing arctic tundra and each other. Hot in pursuit, and not wanting to be excluded from the fun, were people brandishing lethal weapons made out of stone just like Maine people now like to brandish guns. For about two thousand years there was much feasting and happiness, but then catastrophe struck. It got a lot warmer and many of the animals became extinct. The tundra was re-placed by inedible trees. Mainers scratched, scrimped and saved and somehow managed to survive, just as they do now.

EUROPEANS INVADE MAINE

Catastrophe struck again. During the sixteenth and seventeenth centuries, pale men in big and clumsy ships sailed to Maine. Mainers, who have always been a generous people, opened their hearts and gave the palefaces whatever they wanted. The palefaces showed their appreciation by raping, kidnapping and murdering their new-found friends and stealing their land.

KINGS FIGHT KINGS FIGHT KINGS

Pretty soon Maine got so crowded that the palefaces began to fight amongst themselves. On one side were the French, who used Jesuit priests as shields. On the other side were the rogues and villains of the mightiest nation on earth, tiny England. The original Mainers, caught in the middle between all the hatred and ill-will, went crazy and destroyed whatever hadn't been in Maine before 1600.

ALTERNATIVES TO WAR

It should not be assumed that all people did back then was fight. Some colonial couples managed to make love, but unfortunately some were not married. Usually, it was the woman and not the man who was punished. Whipping post, branding iron and death were some of the sentences.

THE WARS GO ON

In 1763, the Peace of Paris was signed and now only one king ruled Maine. Mainers hoped this king would be different from the rest, but he was worse. He taxed everything in sight and made it impossible for anyone but himself and his cronies to get rich. As a result, war was declared against the king and lots of pale and red faces got killed. When it was all over there was no more king for Maine. In his place was a republic, but the leaders of this republic and their cronies were rich, too, and everyone else, including most pale and all red faces in Maine, was still poor.

CAUGHT IN
THE MIDDLE AGAIN

After the war, Maine was surrounded by unfriendly neighbors. To the north were the defeated British. They set up camp in New Brunswick and pointed their guns across the border. To the south was Massachusetts. It owned Maine, taxed everything in sight, and Boston got rich off Maine, carrying on the old tradition. In a political deal, Massachusetts sold two million acres of Maine to one of the richest men in the world, William Bingham, for only pennies an acre. This deal set the tone for generations of land thefts in Maine.

Chamber of Justice

During the War of 1812, the British occupied Bangor. At one point some British officers attempted to take over the Martin Kinsley house in nearby Hampden to use as a headquarters. The lady of the house, however, barricaded it against them and would not answer their poundings at the door. Finally, to be rid of them, she emptied the contents of a chamberpot on the officers' heads. Emptying chamberpots on people's heads thereafter became a favorite Maine joke, still frequently enjoyed with hearty gales of laughter from all concerned. An individual can easily be identified as "from away" if he doesn't laugh heartily when a chamberpot is dumped on his head.

JEFFERSON PUNISHES MAINE

In spite of the fact that Mainers worked harder than anyone else, few got rich. In 1807, President Thomas Jefferson announced an embargo which made it illegal to trade with foreigners. The embargo was valiantly defied by many Mainers, especially those around Eastport, but the rich shipping magnates in Southern Maine complied and the Maine economy was ruined. By the time the law was repealed in 1809, sixty percent of Mainers along the coast were unemployed. Thomas Jefferson voodoo dolls were very popular.

THE YEAR OF
EIGHTEEN-HUNDRED-AND-
FROZE-TO-DEATH

Just about the time when things were beginning to look up, another catastrophe struck. This was the famous winter of 1816 which would have been all right except that it happened during the summer. Crops were ruined and many people starved. Practically the entire state of Maine moved to Ohio. But, once everyone got there, they saw how boring and flat it was, so many trudged back to Maine and started to pick up the pieces again.

MAINE BECOMES MAINE

The biggest piece to be picked up was statehood. In 1819, after thirty-four years of petitions and referendums and manifestos, Mainers voted to separate from Massachusetts. Bay staters were too busy hoarding their money to notice, so there was no protest from them. One year later, the United States Congress gave its approval, but only on the condition that slavery be extended into Missouri. Many Maine people felt guilty about this and became abolitionists.

WAR IN THE WOODS

Now Maine was its own master and had its own wars to worry about. Most noteworthy of its enemies in the early years was the lordly pine. The war against the pine was probably the most popular war ever fought in Maine and is still the subject of much romantic reminiscing. The innocent pine was defenseless against an extremely well-organized onslaught of axes and saws. The only way it could fight back was with massive acts of civil disobedience called log jams, a tactic taught to the pines by the noted advocate of nonviolent resistance, Henry David Thoreau. The log jams did little to turn the tide of the war, however, and served only to immortalize the river drivers who died fighting them.

"BLOODLESS" WAR

The pine was a popular foe elsewhere. The citizens of New Brunswick also declared war against it and snuck over into Aroostook County to do battle. The citizens of Aroostook were furious at the trespass, and for a while it looked as if the pine would be spared and people would kill each other instead. But everyone soon saw there was no money to be made in this war, so the whole thing was called off. Daniel Webster and Lord Ashburton of Great Britain were hired to get drunk and draw up an Aroostook-New Brunswick border. Although it looked a bit crooked, it was tolerated by all.

CIVIL WAR

Just when it looked like Maine was going to have some peace, the Civil War broke out. Feeling guilty about its role in the Missouri Compromise of 1820, and always restless for a good fight, Maine sacrificed more of its native sons per capita (over nine thousand) than any other state in the North. After the war, monuments to these brave young men were erected in nearly every village square.

ESCAPE-VALVE STATE

After the Civil War, Maine was invaded by pale-faced, upper-class elites who were fleeing from the poisonous East Coast cities that their businesses had polluted. On islands such as Mount Desert, they introduced luxuries, class distinctions and vices that were courageously resisted by the native population. Maine was viewed by these outsiders as the perfect place to forget the troubles of the world. They and other like-minded individuals eventually bought up almost all of the Maine coast and erected barricades so that no one else could get in. This influx of alien blood has given Maine the legacy of having more millionaires per poor folk than any other state.

INDUSTRY'S DEMISE

At the beginning of statehood, it looked as if Maine's vast natural resources would eventually make it the richest state in the East. A number of developments after the Civil War put to rest such fantasy. The invention of steel ships sounded the knell for Maine's wooden-ship yards, previously number one in the world. Motorized refrigeration, although a dandy of a convenience, destroyed the Kennebec ice industry. Structural steel, concrete and other modern building materials made Maine lumber less valuable. Maine's once-great textile industry packed up its bags and went South where labor was even cheaper than in Maine. The paper companies were the only major new industry to come to Maine at this time, but not everyone was enthusiastic about them because they dammed and polluted the rivers, killing the fish.

Beauty in the eyes of the stockholder: Paper companies reduced Maine's forest to patchwork

In the twentieth century, war became big business in Maine

THE TWENTIETH CENTURY

Although the new century brought many changes to Maine, people remained poor while out-of-state-owned companies got rich. The paper companies continued to dominate the landscape. They bought the upper half of Maine and began clear-cutting the hell out of it in a desperate race to get to the trees before the spruce budworm. Pesticides were sprayed on the woods, potatoes, blueberries, apples and any organic farmers who got in the way. The industrial giants hired influential lawyers to lobby the Maine legislature to pass laws and tax breaks in their favor. The automobile was introduced and it introduced millions of tourists, fouled up the air, destroyed the railroads and steamboats and killed thousands of people. Fancy superhighways were cut through some of Maine's most productive and beautiful land, and farmers were left homeless and ruined. Hazardous waste dumps and ground-water pollution become commonplace. Fast-food joints, factory outlets, tourist traps and land speculators multiplied faster than anyone could keep track of. Loring Air Force Base's B-52 bombers threatened to be the cause of us being blown up at any minute. In short, "Vacationland" was born.

NOT WITH A WHIMPER, BUT WITH A...

But Mainers were a hardy lot and continued to work hard and pray for the best. There were also plenty of new wars to fight in and weapons to be made. By the time World War II ended, the Pentagon had become a very big industry in Maine, a position that solidified as Cold War tensions mounted. Companies such as the Bath Iron Works were held up as a paragon. The Cold War was good for business and business intended to keep it that way. Mainers could only hope that things wouldn't heat up too bad and finish off Maine as it had begun — with a bang.

GREAT MOMENTS IN VACATIONLAND HISTORY

"Of all the northern quarters of the Union, Maine is that which will increase the fastest."
— *American Encyclopedia, 1808*

1498 John Cabot claims Maine for the King of England even though he never sets foot here.

1566-8 David Ingram walks from the Gulf of Mexico to Maine and writes a book about it when he returns to Europe. Book describes Norumbega, city of riches, at site of present-day Bangor. This marks the beginning of the Maine myth.

1638 John Josselyn visits Maine and also writes a book. He says Mainers were "indolent and intemperate; having earned a little money they spent it for a strong drink, and would not work as hired laborers until it was all spent."

1653 Massachusetts commissioners order people of Wells, Saco and Cape Porpoise to "make sufficient roads within their towns from house to house, and clear and fit them for foot and cart travel." This forced labor marks the beginning of Maine resentment of bossy Massachusetts.

1710 *Nottingham Galley*, three months out of London, piles up on the ledges off Boon Island (near Kennebunkport). When the ship's carpenter died, the survivors ate him, provisions were so scarce.

1748 Inscription in Waldoboro's Old German cemetery: "This town was settled in 1748 by Germans who immigrated to this place with the promise and expectation of finding a prosperous city, instead of which they found nothing but wilderness."

1820 Residents of Augusta try without success to drag Cushnoc Island from the Kennebec River because navigation near it is hazardous. Mill chains are fastened around the island and linked with a team of a hundred oxen. Oxen pull, but get thrown back into the river. The island is still there. Early commentators see this incident as saying something about the Maine character.

1828 William Ladd, who opposed building the Bunker Hill monument on the grounds that it was vanity, founds the American Peace Society in Minot. (Peaceniks in Maine have a long tradition.)

1828 The United States Arsenal is established in Augusta "for the safekeeping of arms and munitions of the United States for the northern and eastern frontier." There is enough firepower to blow up Augusta many times over. (Militarism in Maine has a long tradition.)

1834-36 Land speculation at its height in Bangor. Land which sold for pennies in the morning sells for dollars in the afternoon. In June, 1835, it is rumored that "one evening last week, two paupers escaped from the Bangor almshouse, and though they were caught early the next morning, yet in the meantime, before they were secured, they had made $1,800 each by speculating in timber lands."

1838 U.S. Congressman Jonathan Cilley of Thomaston becomes the last man in the United States to be killed in a duel.

1840s John Poor, of Andover, railroad visionary: "The capacity of the human frame for labor is found to be greater in Maine than in Massachusetts or any state, south or west of it..." Beginning of Maine strong-back, weak-brain myth.

1843 Millerites of Hermon give away all their property, put on white ascension robes and gaze toward the heavens, waiting for the second coming...

Putting on the Dog

The only doghouse on the National Register of Historic Places is a highly decorated Gothic Revival doghouse on the Godfrey-Kellogg Estate in Bangor. You may want to take your dog to see it.

1846   Thoreau visits Bangor and writes: "The mission of men there seems to be, like so many busy demons, to drive the forest all out of the country, from every solitary beaver-swamp and mountain-side, as soon as possible."

1850   Year of John Poor's prophecy: "Maine will present at some future day, along her bays and rivers, a line of cities surpassing those which are now upon the shores of the English Channel, or Baltic Sea."

In 1851 Maine was the first state to institute Prohibition because of disgusting scenes such as this

1850   Three-quarters of all laborers living in Lewiston had been born in Ireland.

1850   Bangor is world's leading lumber port. Also very big in taverns and prostitutes.

1862   Henry David Thoreau dies of consumption. The last words he utters are "moose" and "Indian."

1870   Civil War hero Governor Joshua Chamberlain addresses the Maine State Legislature: "She [Maine] reminds me more of the western states than the rest of New England in her condition and needs — a virgin soil, undeveloped powers, vast forests, and vigorous men, but no money" (and no women, either, judging by his description).

1875   Eastport proclaimed Sardine Capital of the World, and it smells like it.

1876   Capital punishment abolished in Maine, but resurrection of those already executed proves impossible.

1882   "Oscar Wilde, on his American tour, made his only stop in Maine at the Bangor House, en route to New Brunswick. He spoke before an audience in a hall appropriately decorated with sunflowers, and was considerably booed and hissed by the vulgarly curious. It is recorded that no respectable young lady, no matter what her claims to being one of the intelligentsia, was permitted to attend the gathering."[1]

1883   Capital punishment re-established in Maine.

1885   Entrepreneur Luther Maddocks tows a sixty-foot humpback whale into Portland Harbor. He charges the curious to see it and makes $800. Then he sells it for $150 to a company that strips it of its hide and blubber. Whatever is left that can't be used is towed to sea and sunk.

But the carcass gets gas, floats to the surface and drifts into Portland again. People are not amused and tow it out to sea. But the carcass floats back in. This happens over and over again until it comes ashore at Old Orchard Beach. Here it is exhibited as a "sea serpent." People come for miles around to spend their money to see it. After everyone has had their fill, the directors of a Middle West museum purchase the bones for their collection.

1887   Capital punishment abolished again. Resurrection still proves impossible.

1896-8   Great Quoddy Gold Swindle. Rev. Prescott Ford Jernegan and "engineer" Charles Fisher build Electrolyc Marine Salts Company in Lubec. At its peak, company employs seven hundred and makes gold from sea water at phenomenal rates: $350,000 worth of shares are bought by public overnight. Jernegan and Fisher skip town with money and everyone loses his shirt. Investigation reveals gold-making machines were fed each night with gold by Fisher when no one else was looking.

1917   An Auburn factory makes seventy-five percent of the world's entire supply of white canvas shoes in this year.

The photograph shows the first day-light parade anywhere of the revived Ku Klux Klan. It took place in Milo, Maine, on Labor Day, 1923. At its peak in the mid-twenties the Klan claimed twenty thousand adherents in the state. History books don't discuss the Klan very much, but it probably was responsible for electing Ralph Owen Brewster governor in 1924. The Klan's pitch in Maine was not so much anti-Negro (darn few of them around) as much as anti-Catholic, anti-Jew, and anti-foreigner. The Klansmen were white, Republican, Protestant teetotalers. Being so afflicted, they desperately needed excitement which the cross-burning Klan could supply.

Courtesy of Sam Pennington

1918   Kaiser Wilhelm's radio message seeking to negotiate an end to World War I with President Wilson is received at the Otter Cliffs Radio Station (Mt. Desert Island).

1920s   "Free love" colony flourishes in Portland.

1931   Shaker community in Alfred closes from lack of new blood. Not surprising, since Shakers practice celibacy.

1947   Loring Air Force Base runway is built directly in line with Main Street, Limestone. When bombers take off the sidewalks vibrate and the air thunders. "The bombers are part of the setting," says town manager Thomas Stevens. "We really don't mind the noise. You sort of get used to it."

1954   Maine becomes the last state in the Union to allow Indians the right to vote.

1954   Steve Riley, *Portland Press Herald* columnist, writes: 'There's little doubt that if the men in the Kremlin are plotting an attack to the U.S. they're singling out Maine for attention."

1955   Addressing complaints that Navy spy planes make too much noise as they land and take off from Brunswick Naval Air Station, Commanding Officer Captain Joseph T. Yavorsky says: "Try to consider this nuisance as your part in the national defense effort. Try to picture those planes with nine to a dozen crew members out over the Atlantic for a nine-hour patrol period, and say a little prayer for their safe return. Maybe it will help you get to sleep more quickly."

The Lewiston-Auburn Shoe Strike of 1937

RED WEDNESDAY

Maine has been about as receptive to labor unions as the average Maine farmer has been to rabid coyotes. When John L. Lewis' CIO led the low-paid, French-Canadian-descent shoe-shop workers of Lewiston and Auburn out on a strike in 1937, the owners of the nineteen mills — most of them in Auburn — brought out their phalanxes of lawyers, their governor, their scabs, their night-stick-wielding police, their National Guard, and their Maine Supreme Court judge who issued an injunction against the strike. The climax of the three-month-long strike was reached when a thousand workers on a Wednesday morning tried to cross the North Bridge from where they lived in Lewiston to where they worked in Auburn. They were met by local and state police who attacked with clubs and tear gas, driving them back. The next day four hundred National Guardsmen set up to repel another march that failed to materialize. The upshot was that the CIO was defeated. A big factor was the opposition of the Roman Catholic priests who denounced the CIO as being penetrated with "Socialists and Communists."

1950s	Hungarian refugees in New Brunswick are harassed by nearby Loring Air Force Base personnel who claim they are Russian spies.
1957	Movie Peyton Place, starring Lana Turner, is filmed in Camden.
1957	A Loring Air Force Base B-52 bomber crashes at Andover, New Brunswick, killing eight of nine aboard.
1958	An Air Force F89H Scorpion jet fighter crashes into a frozen field near Presque Isle, killing the two on board.
1963	The U.S. nuclear attack submarine Thresher sinks on its trial run, killing all 129 men aboard. It was built at Portsmouth-Kittery Naval Shipyard.
1960s	"Our company came to Maine, quite frankly, because we knew there was a large

SO YOU THINK YOU KNOW

1. The Humiliation of Verrazzano: In 1524, Giovanni da Verrazzano, an Italian sailing under the French flag, claimed Maine for France. But the Maine Indians wanted nothing to do with his claim. The Indians shot at his ship with arrows and made obscene gestures including "exhibiting their bare behinds" in his direction.

SO YOU THINK YOU KNOW MAINE MASSACRES:

> The number of Verrazzano's men killed during this incident was
> a) 0
> b) 1
> c) 16
> d) 347
> e) none of the above.

2. Kidnapped! In June, 1605, at the mouth of the St. Georges River, near present-day Port Clyde, five Maine Indians were kidnapped, imprisoned and taken against their will to England aboard the *Archangel* under the command of Captain James Waymouth. This was the first recorded act of treachery against the Maine Indians by the English. Three of the five Indians made it back alive to their families and homes in Maine.

SO YOU THINK YOU KNOW MAINE MASSACRES:

> Tahanedo, Amoret, Skicoworos, Maneddo and Suffacomoit
> a) are the names of five streams in Maine where massacres have occurred.
> b) are the names of five wines in Maine that are bottled near the sites of the massacres.
> c) are the last names of the five most popular players on the Maine Guides minor-league baseball team.
> d) are the names of the five Indians kidnapped by Waymouth.

3. First Dutch Contact: In 1609, while searching for the northwest passage, Henry Hudson hove to in Casco Bay to "repair his storm-battered vessel." After the ship was repaired, Hudson and his men repaid the kindness and hospitality shown them during their misfortune by the Maine Indians by attacking Indian villages and robbing them of their supplies. "We...drove the savages from their houses and took the spoyle of them," is how Hudson's chronicler quaintly described the pillaging.

SO YOU THINK YOU KNOW MAINE MASSACRES:

> *Half Moon* was the name of Hudson's ship. It has been memorialized in Maine by having which of the following named after it?
> a) A river.
> b) A cove.
> c) A motor court in Freeport off I-95.
> d) A baseball team.

4. English Claim All of Maine for Themselves: In 1613, Captain Samuel Argall, under orders from the Virginia Colony, attacked and destroyed the month-old French colony of St. Sauveur at Somes Sound on Mt. Desert Island. Father Gilbert du Thet's death by English musket ball was the first recorded act of violence between the English and French in the New World. This helped set off 150 years of warfare between the two superpowers battling it out for possession of North America.

SO YOU THINK YOU KNOW MAINE MASSACRES:

> After their conquest of St. Sauveur, Argall and his men
> a) went back to Jamestown.
> b) climbed Mt. Cadillac and marvelled at the view.
> c) continued down the coast and destroyed the French settlements at St. Croix and Port Royal.
> d) married Indian princesses and were never heard from again.

force of women with nimble fingers and soft brains here," so says an engineer with computer pioneer Fairchild Digital of South Portland in *The Nation* magazine.

1970 William Hinkley, chief field inspector for the Department of Environmental Protection, remembers: "One of the worst spills I have ever seen happened about five years ago on the Androscoggin River. A valve on the white liquor [concentrated chemicals for the digester] tank at the Oxford Plant [Rumford] broke and 150,000 gallons of white liquor poured right out into the water. I happened to be on a bridge down river from the plant and you could see the suckers trying to crawl out of the river."

Massacres?

5. Indian Plague: Around 1616, Europeans introduced Maine Indians to their diseases. A number of epidemics swept along the coast and thousands of Indians died. A contemporary English report from the Saco River called the epidemic among the Indians "the greatest [mortality] that ever happened within the memory of man."

SO YOU THINK YOU KNOW MAINE MASSACRES:

> Which of the following items, also introduced to the Indians by the Europeans, ripped apart the fabric of their culture and life?
> a) Knives.
> b) Guns.
> c) Private property.
> d) Alcohol.
> e) All of the above.

6. Scientific Experiment on the Saco: In 1675, an Indian woman and her baby boy were out on the Saco River in a canoe. They were approached by a boatload of English sailors who had heard that Indian babies knew how to swim from birth, just like animals. The Englishmen tested out the theory by capsizing the defenseless canoe. The mother dived under and managed to bring up her baby alive, but he soon died. The English sailors did not know the baby was the son of Squando, an Indian chief. The murder of his son helped to touch off King Philip's War in Maine. An estimated six hundred Englishmen and three thousand Indians lost their lives during this war which lasted three years.

SO YOU THINK YOU KNOW MAINE MASSACRES:

> True or False: The high-spirited sailors who tipped over the canoe were brought to trial and punished for their crime.

7. Death of a Legend: In 1724, a band of English mercenaries under the command of Jeremiah Moulton and Johnson Harmon attacked the Indian village/Jesuit mission at Norridgewock on the Kennebec River. At least eighty Indians were killed by the surprise invasion. The primary target of the mission, Father Sebastian Rale, was also killed. For thirty-three years he had been in charge of the mission and was loved by the Indians. After the massacre, Rale's scalp and twenty-six Indian scalps were reportedly taken to Boston and "paraded in victory." (Each Indian scalp was worth one hundred pounds to the victors thanks to a bounty offered by the Massachusetts government. Father Rale's scalp was worth even more.)

SO YOU THINK YOU KNOW MAINE MASSACRES:

> True or false: After the English were gone, some of the surviving Indians returned to the ruins of the village and found Father Rale shot in a thousand places, scalped, his skull broken to pieces with the blows of hatchets, his mouth and eyes full of mud, the bones of his legs fractured, and all of his members mangled in a hundred different ways.

8. Is Portland Burning? On October 16, 1775, Captain Henry Mowatt of the British sloop-of-war *Canceau* opened fire on the site of present-day Portland: 414 buildings went up in flames and two thousand people were left homeless.

SO YOU THINK YOU KNOW MAINE MASSACRES:

Mowatt destroyed Portland because
a) he was under orders to do so.
b) he was once held as a prisoner there and sought revenge.
c) he was a pyromaniac.
d) there was a war going on between the English and the thirteen colonies and he wanted to make sure Mainers knew about it.
e) all of the above.

1972   The first environmental impact statement issued by the Air Force about the proposed Over-the-Horizon Radar admits that leveling all the trees and shrubs from the seven-hundred-acre Somerset County site "could cause disruption of wildlife."

1973   The Portsmouth-Kittery Naval Shipyard is number one on the Navy's list of inefficient yards.

SO YOU THINK YOU KNOW

Maine Massacres?

9. The Massacre of the Northern Penguin: The great auk was a large, flightless bird that looked like the Southern Hemisphere's penguin. Millions used to nest on the offshore islands of the North Atlantic, such as Maine's own Matinicus Rock. By the late 1700s, millions of pounds of auk eggs, meat, oil, down and feathers were being shipped each year to European markets.

SO YOU THINK YOU KNOW MAINE MASSACRES:
   The great auk, now extinct,
   a)   is the Maine state bird.
   b)   used to spend its winters in Jamaica and listen to reggae music.
   c)   used to eat puffins.
   d)   is the name of Maine's number-one punk rock band.
   e)   used to mate and nest in large social groups.

10. *Rangifer Tarandus* Bids Adieu to Maine: The woodland caribou, also known as "the American reindeer," weighs between two hundred and four hundred pounds and used to number in the thousands in Maine. But they were over-hunted and couldn't adapt to the "cutover, second-growth forest left in the wake of loggers and farmers." The last reliable sighting of native caribou in Maine was in 1908.

SO YOU THINK YOU KNOW MAINE MASSACRES:

Paralaphostrongylus
   a)   is the scientific name for caribou antlers.
   b)   is a parasite carried by deer that is fatal to caribou.
   c)   is the name of a dinosaur, now extinct, that was an ancestor of the caribou.
   d)   is the name of a famous Penobscot Indian which translated means "he who runs like the caribou."
   e)   all of the above.

Answers: 1:a; 2:d; 3:c; 4:c; 5:e; 6: false; 7: true (according to Charlevoix); 8:e; 9:e; 10:b.

1973   Five killed as Brunswick Naval Air Station P-3 plane crashes into the Gulf of Maine forty miles south of Brunswick.

1975   During a three-week period, sightings of UFOs over Loring Air Force Base occur. During this time, eleven nuclear bomber bases in the northern part of the country declare top-level security alerts.

In 1983, The Citizens Against UFO Secrecy attempt to get 135 documents relating to the UFO sightings released under the Freedom of Information Act. The judge in the case says the documents were so sensitive that their release would jeopardize the nation's security. The FBI, the FAA, the North American Air Defense Command, the Army, Navy and Air Force have witheld information on the sightings.

1976   President Ford announces an eighty percent cutback at Loring Air Force Base. People panic. Real estate prices go down, retail sales drop, investors pull out of deals. Peaceniks talk of "conversion" of Aroostook economy to basket weaving.

Severin Beliveau, prominent Democratic lobbyist and Senator William S. Cohen, Republican, lead charge of a well-financed "Save Loring" lobby. Under intense pressure, President Carter annuls the cutbacks in 1979, and announces a new building program including a second runway. Property values jump, retail sales rise and investors are eager to get in on deals. Peaceniks stop talking about basket weaving.

1978   Closest yet. Crash of Brunswick Naval Air Station P-3 plane misses Poland Springs house by less than a hundred yards and kills all eight aboard.

1979   John Lennon and Yoko Ono go house-hunting in North Harpswell, but decide they like New York City better.

1981   Brigadier General E.G. Shuler, commander at Loring Air Force Base, says: "Today if Soviet submarines fired missiles in a surprise attack, much of my alert force could not get off the ground before the [incoming] missiles hit."

1982   Twelve thousand mice are gassed to death by the Jackson Lab of Bar Harbor during the first week of the air traffic controllers' strike. The world's largest producer of mice explains by saying that the mice had been ordered by researchers from around the

Photo by Dept. of the Army, Corps of Engineers

The Presque Isle Air Force Base (now a commercial airport) owns the little-known distinction of being the location of the first American intercontinental missiles aimed at the Soviet Union. Called the SNARK (rhymes with shark), these sixty-seven-foot-long missiles were mounted on mobile launchers and had a range of five thousand miles, but were terribly inaccurate (people in Greenland are probably glad they were never used). New missile technology forced this, the only Snark facility ever constructed in the country, to shut down in 1962, almost before it was completed.

country but were unable to be shipped out on the day promised because of the strike. The researchers order mice of specific age and weight and the difference of a day in receiving the mice is critical and can ruin an experiment. "Mice don't have any shelf life," says Jackson Lab animal resources administrative officer John L. Dorey.

1982 Vice President George Bush eats lunch at MacLean's Restaurant in Brunswick. "I would guess that there were around fifty security people, not counting all the local and state cops who parked up and down the street," says owner Scott MacLean.

1983 Three years into the new draft law, Maine ranks second-highest in the nation in complying with it: 96.1% of Maine's eighteen-year-olds who are supposed to register have done so.

1983 Defense contractors who have already contributed to the 1984 re-election "war chest" of Senator William S. Cohen are: Litton Industries, Bath Iron Works, Hughes Air Craft, Boeing Air Craft, Northrop Aircraft, General Electric, Raytheon and General Dynamics. As a member of the Senate Armed Services Committee, Senator Cohen has intercourse with these firms frequently.

1983 William Spademan, Sarah Schmidt, Tamora Goltz and David Stimson declare their house in Brunswick a nuclear-free zone. They demand that their home be taken off the target lists of any government which has nuclear weapons or which is considering getting them. They haven't been bombed as of the publication of this book.

1983 Thirty years previous there were over 160

What Are Two Steam Locomotives Doing on the Allagash?

Rusting. There once was a sixteen-mile log-hauling railway from Umbazooksus Lake to the strip of land between Eagle and Chamberlain Lake. The locomotives were brought there overland in the winter fifty miles from Canada on sledges. Next time you're on the Allagash and feel like you've gotten away from it all, scout around a little and you'll find these two huge locomotives. This general practice can be pursued throughout the whole of the Maine woods, which has been used as a dumping ground by logging companies for over a hundred years. The practice was just to leave the junk — from piles of cans to machinery to locomotives — and move on to level the next section of woods.

farms raising potatoes from Portage to Oxbow. Now there are four in Ashland, none in Portage and none in Oxbow.

1983   About 125 members of Brewer's First Apostolic Church burn books, rock albums, t-shirts and other "works of the devil" at a church service.

1983   Casco Bay tidal flats finally declared free of oil pollution eleven years after 100,000-gallon oil spill by the tanker M.V. Tamano. However, most of the flats remain closed because of the "continued presence of bacterial pollution from sewer effluents."

1983   Two former members of Orono's Junior Firefighters' Squad admit in district court they were responsible for fifty-five cases of arson in Orono during 1978.

1983   A cow, raised on a farm in Turner, sells for $530,000 at a New York City auction. Cow's name: Dreamstreet Rorae Poco-hontis.

1984   Family Planning of Maine releases figures which show that fifty-one percent of all the AFDC (Aid to Families with Dependent Children) payments in Maine in 1981 went to teenagers.

NOTE
1. Maine, A Guide Downeast, Federal Writers' Project, Works Progress Administration, Houghton Mifflin, Boston, 1937, p. 137.

Gus Gannett Newspapers

In the 1960 Presidential election, Richard Nixon outpolled John F. Kennedy in Maine largely because of the popularity of Maine's Republican Senator, Margaret Chase Smith, also on the ballot, for re-election to the Senate that year.

"You've heard of people riding on a candidate's coattails," Nixon remarked in a speech in Bangor, "Here in Maine we're hanging on as hard as we can to Margaret's skirts."

In the picture above, the Senator from Maine is shown presenting Nixon with the bill from her tailor for the skirts Nixon tore that had to be mended.

RUSSIANS! In Richmond.

In 1951 the town of Richmond was in sad shape — farms were abandoned and many houses were in disrepair. A Russian count with the Prussian name of Von Pushenthal came to the area, saw the desolation and opportunity, and advertised in the emigre newspapers. He said that Richmond was like Russia, both the land and the climate. So they came — somewhere between five hundred and a thousand families who settled in or near Richmond.

Most were second-wave immigrants who had been in German-occupied sections of the Soviet Union and retreated with the Germans. They made it to the Displaced Person camps and eventually to America, although some were first-wave immigrants who had been out of Russia since the Revolution.

When the Russians, Byelorussians, Ukrainians and Balts first came they didn't have much in the way of worldly goods. A group of Quakers from nearby towns came to make a survey for the purpose of donating goods to these poor people. They were met with great hostility, and most of the immigrants, no matter how needy, refused to cooperate. When the gentle Quakers were rejected in their good works, they couldn't figure out why. Finally, someone told them that the new people thought they were secret police! The survey stopped.

Mark Melnicove

INDIANS WIN LAND CLAIMS,

BUT LOSE AT BINGO

Although Maine's tiny Penobscot and Passamaquoddy Indian tribes successfully faced down the state and federal governments in a high-stakes land-claims lawsuit (they got $54.5 million to buy three hundred thousand acres of land and another $27 million in cash in the 1980 settlement), the Penobscots weren't so fortunate when they tried to buck Maine's antigambling laws.

Since 1976 the Penobscots had been holding higher-and-higher-stakes bingo games in a hall on Indian Island north of Bangor. The hall was also decorated with slot machines. Up to six hundred people used to play the games — on Sundays, too, no less — and the bingo jackpots went up to $10,000.

All this was very illegal according to Maine law, but the Indians said they didn't have to abide by white man's law, being Indians on the reservation. Although people came from hundreds of miles to play, the Indians said it was "an internal tribal matter." During the legal proceedings, threats appeared in the press that little old ladies would hold the state police at bay on the Indian Island bridge should the judgement be adverse to the Indians.

But when the adverse judgement came — from the U.S. Supreme Court — no little old ladies appeared on the bridge and the Penobscots announced plans to build a $2.5-million gambling hall on Pequot Indian property in Connecticut — surprising, however, some Pequots who said it was news to them.

Culmination of Maine history: Edmund S. Muskie received first extra-terrestrial communication in early 1984

2 Tourist Traps

wo million people from out of state come to the center of Maine's tourist industry — L.L. Bean's. That is two million a year. It seems about two million stop at Maine people's houses afterwards — these are long-lost acquaintances — for supper and a nice free bed. Maine people have nothing against L.L. Bean's except they don't make enough of their own stuff. Nor do they dirty their hands by selling guns. This would bring the real sportsmen a little too close to the nonsports who make up most of the clientele. The Casco Bay Shirt wouldn't look good on the typical bear hunter.

According to sources in the shipping department, many of the products that dewy-eyed tourists come to Maine to buy are made in various foreign parts. One might think from being in the store that everything is whipped up out back when the clerk goes to get the thing in your size. Nothing could be further from the truth. Many items are shipped in from all over the world to the great warehouses you see on your right when you come into town from the south. These are then shipped from the post office to points all over the world with the Freeport, Maine, postmark like they were from a cabin in the backwoods. But Bean's is really a slick, computer-controlled merchandise mart. This is not primarily a camping store — it is a store for people who want to *look* like they are camping or hunting or, at least, getting ready for muggers on the streets of New York.

The final straw for many in the destruction of the L.L. Bean's outdoor image came when it supported with many dollars the Maine Yankee Atomic Power Plant during the shutdown referenda. This could not be the act of an industry that is concerned about the Maine environment.

* * * * * *

In the museum trade, there is a term which applies to private, rather scandalous attractions. They are called snake farms. There are not many of these in Maine, for we only have a few kinds of

ALTERNATIVE #1 TO L.L. BEAN

Mark Melnicove

Quality boots at very low prices can be obtained at Pushards at South Gardiner on the Kennebec, just up the road from the huge Associated Grocers warehouse. You will have to pick your way literally through piles of footgear, but there is a coal stove to get warm with. This establishment wins the prize for the most unpretentious shoe store in Maine.

Gui Gannett Newspapers

Typical scene at Old Orchard Beach

nonpoisonous snakes, but one of the most out-standing is on Route 1 in Belfast — Perry's Nut House. It is a collection, on the outside, of funky, painted wooden animals and, on the inside, of stuffed this and that along with cashews and guava jelly for sale.

It is here that the young of midcoast Maine come to get in touch with the outer world. They see their first pair of ratty-looking bear cubs, boxing; the first stuffed alligator; the first hammerhead shark. It is here that a rather seedy collection of nuts first raises the specter of Zanzibar or Malaysia. This wooden-floored store of the bizarre serves as a low-rated natural history museum for those who can't make it to New York or Washington.

Where the Smithsonian overwhelms, Perry's serves just the right size on a Sunday afternoon ride. For here we have, in a tired and muffled way, the essence of the foreign world. Besides, one cannot buy such delicious white chocolate in those more esteemed and distant museums.

What Maine needs is more, not fewer, snake farms where children can see on their own terms the mysterious hokeyness of life. Perhaps snakes could be imported from Florida and Texas. A huge rock collection might be made available in the middle of the shoppes in Camden, or a heated alligator-wrestling farm and pool in Kennebunkport to keep so many Maine people from going to Florida in the winter. Florida is filled with snake farms, such as Busch Gardens and the Epcot Center. Maine should have some of these attractions. We frequently bemoan the pressure the tourists put on the coastal roads in July and August. Why not a Disney World in Farmington or a Williamsburg at the Forks? If one Wedding Cake House brings thousands to town, just think what Wedding Cakeland will do! It is a question of vision.

The title, tourist trap, has real meaning. We want to entice and hold, like a woodchuck in a Havaheart, the tourist to our bosom, at least until all our strength is gone or all his money. What more besides snake farms could Maine do to make both coast and inland more attractive to the tourist? Why not gambling?

In Maine, the climate is set for more and bigger gambling halls. We have bingo, we have horse racing, and we have a state lottery. Travelers play roulette and cards on the ferry to Nova Scotia. Why not slot machines in every grocery, gambling clubs in every port? Just think of the hotels one could build on Monhegan. Maine would be a gambler's paradise. The slots in Bass Wayside could squeeze out every last nickel. Airports would expand, the job market would triple and taxes go down. Just think of Wayne Newton singing at Sugarloaf! Think of the employment for Maine's Potato and Lobster Queens!

Mark Melnicove

Typical warm-hearted Yankee welcome along the Maine coast

MAINE IS SPELLED MAINE

ME ME ME
Down in old Floriday
there's a river called Kissimee;
it's the same thing we say to the girls
in the Grand State of Maine, kiss-i-ME!
Now Maine's old Tourist Board
likes to say spend it on ME,
because it's the only money
us Maineiacs ever get to see.
But if we miss the tourist deal
all we can say is Kick ME!
And scream all the way to the poor house
where we feed on soup made of pea.
This prompts us to get religion,
but not a bible-banging spree;
we go to the First Unitarian Church of Kittery, Maine,
better known as _ _ _ _ _ * ME.

*Heavens! Is the *Uncensored Guide* censored?
No, it's just more fun if *you* fill in the blanks.

Maine Gifts*

STUFFED PUFFIN — A delightful little rare bird with a colorful beak, guaranteed to be from Matinicus Rock. Shot with an airgun to avoid damaging the feathers. Only $495.00. Available from Maine Audubon Society.

ANDRE THE SEAL KEY RINGS — Guaranteed to return to you if lost, $3.95 for regular, $6.95 for the underwater model.

BLACK BEAUTY LOBSTER PINS — Three-inch pin of coal washed ashore from the schooner *Thelma Prout*. Handcarved by Maine fishermen's wives. This little pin captures the true beauty of *Homarus americanus*. $46.95.

TWENTY-POUND FIR BALSAM PILLOW — Made specifically for city dwellers. A pillow this size is guaranteed to outcompete the odors of garbage drifting up from city streets. $56.95.

BEACH-GLASS MAKER — A motorized bronze cylinder can turn your old beer and Vaseline bottles into beautiful and even valuable beach glass. Comes complete with rocks, sand and seawater. Runs on house current, very quiet. $129.95.

APPLE MAKER — Converts apple cider back into apples that are stem- and seed-free. Makes twenty MacIntosh or ten Baldwin apples from each full gallon. $79.95

COUNTRY EDITOR'S KIT — Just the toy for the budding journalist. Consists of pithy sayings and old etchings that can be arranged to make a nice little newspaper for friends and family. Press optional. Kit alone $4.95; with old-fashioned press and type $3,495 (shipping weight 2,648 lb.; you pay shipping charges).

FAMOUS METINIC BRAND SEAGULL STEW — Cans of hearty herring gull or Arctic (black back) gull stew. Sure to put hair on your chest, man or woman. A delightfully fishy undertaste that makes two meals in one. Made with Maine seagulls, Maine potatoes, Maine milk and Maine salt — only the pepper is imported. $24.00 for the case of one dozen No. 10 cans (guaranteed not to be dump gulls).

A survey of interesting gifts available along Route 1.

ALTERNATIVE #2 TO L.L. BEAN

If you like to support a huge, impersonal corporation that expressed its environmental concern by donating a fortune to defeat the referenda to shut down the Maine Yankee Atomic Power Plant, then go ahead and shop at L.L. Bean, located in the Freeport Rich Trade Zone. But an alternative preferred by Real Maine People is Povich's in downtown Bath, a mom-and-pop operation since 1910, where the service is not canned, and the offerings include men's garters, overalls, coveralls, and blanket-lined frocks. Located at 143 Front St.

Mark Melnicove

Typical view of Central Park Maine (to the left)

Central Park, Maine

New Yorkers are always bragging about their Central Park, but Maine has a Central Park, too, and it beats New York's by miles — many miles.

Central Park in Maine is the I-95 median strip. This grassy knoll of rocks, bushes and trees stretches the full 303 miles from Kittery to Houlton. New Yorkers will note that their park is puny in comparision. Aesthetically, Maine's park also comes out on top. I-95's serpentine form is much more pleasing to the eye than New York's boring rectangle.

In their favor, New York park-goers have a better selection of food. They can choose from a wide variety of international cuisines at park concession stands. Park-goers in Maine must be content with roadkill (if they can beat the crows to it) and edible weeds (if they can stomach the accumulated auto-diesel exhaust and highway pesticides and salts).

The pitiful selection of food in Central Park Maine is more than offset by the terrifying New York crime statistics. As most Maine natives know, people who walk into Central Park New York never come out alive. But it's only the

pedestrians who *leave* Central Park Maine and wander onto I-95 that run the risk of getting killed.

Actually, most Mainers prefer to savor the sights and sounds of their park while driving past it. (In fact, it may be illegal to do otherwise.) Park designers took this native habit into consideration. It is therefore possible to see all of Maine's park in the six hours it takes to drive it. Thanks to traffic jams, it also takes New Yorkers six hours to drive the length of their park. Tragically, they see far less of their park this way, and it makes them wish they were in Maine.

In defense of their park, New Yorkers point out that Central Park Maine is a cultural wasteland. The few art objects placed in the park, such as Central Maine Power Co.'s Extra High Voltage wires and towers, cannot compare to the majesty on display in the Metropolitan Museum of Art. In addition, New Yorkers charge that the Maine State Police severely limit access to the park with their "Authorized Vehicles Only" signs, a practice virtually unheard of even in lawless New York City.

3 Maine Eats & Drinks

The meat thermometer is not known in Maine. Butchers bemoan the treatment given the fine cuts of meat by Maine cooks. As with the British, meat is always overdone — the color of shoe leather and only slightly softer.

As for dining out, about the only place in Maine of any note is Helen's Restaurant in Machias. There, for under two dollars, you can get a quarter of a pie. The pie is not only bigger but sweeter, and the load of sugar will keep you going on your trip through the blueberry barrens. But aside from Helen's — and a few other places — it is almost impossible to get a good meal dining out at anything approaching a decent price. Generally, if you want a good meal you'll have to cook it yourself. Of course there is only one cookbook that should be used in Maine — *Fanny Farmer*. Oh, there might be a local recipe in the church cookbook for jellied salad or fifty-dollar-prize molasses, but generally it must be *FF*.

Naturally, beans are the center of the perfect Maine meal, which should have as accompaniment Grandma's yeast rolls, Kirschner natural-casing franks, pineapple cole slaw, chow-chow (green tomato relish), large tumblers of milk, Graham cracker pie. This was what one of the authors had growing up in his grandmother's home, and if it is good enough for him, it is good enough for you.

There is one other meal that might compete: lobster stew, whole-wheat biscuits, Original Trenton Oyster Crackers, a small dish of rabbit food (if desired) and a light sponge pie for dessert. Either of these meals will cause out-of-staters to move in with you, so use them judiciously.

If you don't want to go to the trouble of baking beans some Saturday, the nearest substitute is the local bean supper at a church or grange hall. Some of these are very good but others are not. Never go to a bean supper at a Mormon Church, for they will make a pitch and, unless you want to be converted, you'll be sorry.

One of the biggest questions in the annual slaughter of lobsters in the summer is whether it hurts them to be boiled or steamed in the old lobster kettle. News from the researchers at Woods Hole, Massachusetts, is that it sure

BAKED BEANS

Surely, as time goes by,
no one will know how to bake
that noble bean, kidney, yellow eye, or pea,
and out of packages will come all the cake.
That old tradition of baking your own
is going by the boards,
what with sushi, tofu and fried rice —
Good Ol' Satiddy Night will be missed by hordes.
Best of all was cuddling up,
on a cold fall evening
as the gas warmed up the sheets
and blasted holes in the weavin'.
So, bring back beans,
bring back molasses,
bring back salt pork, mustard and onions,
so we'll have something to please our asses!

Mark Melnicove

Topsham Dairy Queen made famous by President Lyndon Baines Johnson

enough does. Photographs taken with electron microscopes show sensitive little hairs grow all over the shell which just looks hard to us. When they squirm and scramble in the pot, you know they are feeling awful pain. If that doesn't bother you, go ahead and eat them with a little butter and lemon and mayonnaise and cheap bread (to make a sandwich Metinic Island style). Incidentally, no native Mainer can eat lobsters in a restaurant unless forced to. They have to be eaten on a picnic table spread with newspapers — to properly sop up the slop. And they have to be *steamed*, not boiled!

Besides lobster and beans, the big product in Maine is spuds. The quality of Maine potatoes is in doubt these days. Frequent letters to the Maine newspapers claim the superiority of California or Idaho spuds in size, cleanliness and freedom from rot. Maine farmers plow along stubbornly fighting every attempt to clean up their act and lose more and more of the out-of-state and even the Maine markets.

Doughnuts are the ultimate Maine fruit — said to have been invented by a Captain Crockett of Rockport who had been to Europe and seen the bagel. The Maine doughnut usually tends to be sweeter and more cakelike. The doughnut has inspired many poems

Doughnuts at their very best are fresh and crispy on the outside, sweet with cinnamon and nutmeg, and slightly chewy on the inside. Whether doughnuts like this are available on the current market is questionable. Some claim the last good commercial doughnut made was in Schwartz's Sweet Shoppe in Fort Fairfield in 1974. What with croissants making their way into the state, it is not inconceivable that some young cook will take up the challenge and make a truly good doughnut again.

As for coffee, the less said the better for all. Most Maine cooks boil the hell out of the stuff, and it tastes terrible. A slight improvement has appeared in the quality of diner coffee with the appearance of the new-style coffee machines. The giant old pressure steamers produced some of the worst brew possible. Home coffee-brewing has rapidly improved with the advent of gourmet shoppes with Mocha and Java for six dollars a pound and with home coffee grinders, but most Maine people think this stuff is only for "foreigners."

A Maine Man's Heaven...

A Cool Can of Beer Between the Legs

Maine people drink about twenty-six million gallons of beer each year. That is about twenty-four gallons a year for every man, woman and child in the state. Now, considering that a third of the population are kids, who don't drink much before they are twelve, and another third are teetotalers left over from the days when Maine spearheaded Prohibition with the infamous "Maine Law" passed in 1851, and a small percentage of people (the upper class) drink hard stuff, the *Uncensored Guide* has concluded that there are about a quarter of a million people in this sparsely populated state who drink a six-pack of beer every night including the Sabbath. Of this number, we estimate that about half consume their favorite suds in the privacy of their home or neighborhood tavern, only presenting a menace to the rest of the populace when they drive home from the tavern. (Of course, if we happen to be married to one of these, or are a son or daughter, we constantly are menaced by the famous Maine "back o' the hand," meted out in a drunken rage when Dad finally gets home.)

But the real menace comes because of the old Maine tradition of, not drinking and then driving, but drinking *while* driving — specifically, with a cool can of beer between the legs. Men, especially, like to drive around all evening drinking. It is one of their major forms of recreation, punctuated with obscene yelling at women. They conclude at 3 a.m. with high-speed chases on icy roads with the local, county, and state constabulary (this being *their* favorite form of recreation). The *Uncensored Guide* estimates that each night in Maine, given three drunks to a car, there are approximately forty-two thousand (42,000) of these drunken drivers on the road.

Your best bet for self-preservation is not to go out in your car — or even as a pedestrian — after sundown.

Mark Melnicove

Typical sophisticated bar in Portland's
Old Port-Exchange Street area

Top Three Hard Stuff in Maine

1. **Allen's Coffee Brandy**
2. **Bacardi Silver Rum**
3. **Canadian LTD Whiskey**

Other big sellers, according to the state Bureau of Alcoholic Beverages, include Seagram's Seven Blended Whiskey (traditionally drunk with ginger ale) and Popov and Five O'Clock Vodka (both traditionally injected with hypodermic needle).

The placement of Allen's Coffee Brandy was an astonishment to the *Uncensored Guide* authors. Who could be drinking all that stuff? The question was resolved when state officials informed us that lobstermen use it as a preservative for their bait.

Typical Maine Recipes

CHICKADEE FRICASSEE

The chickadee is the Maine State Bird. Much has been said about its cheery notes around the bird feeder in the winter and its pert little peckings, but many do not know that it is a very fine — if illegal — treat to eat. Gathering the birds can be tiresome, but if one keeps the feeder well stocked and an airgun handy, it is possible to get enough. Since they are such small birds it will take about forty to make a meal for four.

40 whole chickadee breasts, boned
clarified butter
oil
thyme
salt and pepper to taste
a light tomato sauce
Gruyere cheese grated

Saute the chickadee breasts for one and a half minutes per side in a mixture of clarified butter and oil. Place in a large baking pan, cover with tomato sauce and sprinkle with thyme. Bake twenty-five minutes in a 350-degree oven. Remove from oven, sprinkle each breast with cheese and place under the broiler for two minutes or until the cheese melts. Serve with wild rice, fiddleheads and a fine rose wine.

LOBSTER WISCASSET
(Homard au radon)

Choose two fine specimens of mutant lobsters straight from Maine Yankee coolant area. While they are barely alive, cut them in two in the width. Reserve their radioactive liquid. Meltdown a half pound of butter.

Saute the lobster in the butter with two minced onions and one mushroom cloud.

Pour the contents of the saute and the reserved radioactive liquid over the mutant lobsters, which you have transferred to a large lead saucepan. Add a whole squeezed lemon and simmer for thirty half-lives.

Season to taste. Serve in a 7¼-size Civil Defense helmet. Accompany with rice, fiddleheads and a good rose wine.

SEAL OF MAINE STEW

This is not a recipe for seal stew. That sea-loving mammal, though abundant in Maine, is usually eaten only by Eskimo and polar bears. No, this is a stew made from the ingredients on the Great Seal of Maine, which is emblazoned on the state flag.

First of all, there in the center, the chief ingredient, is a moose. Now that killing them is permitted again, it should be easy to obtain. Secondly, there is the pine tree. All the needles from one will do. Then there is a fisherman and a farmer. Since we are not cannibals, the food that these two figures produce will be considered, namely cod and potatoes.

the meat of one moose, shot, dressed, skun and removed from bones. Bones, horns and hooves reserved for stock
the needles of one large pine tree (about 20 bushels)
1 barrel of potatoes
1 salt codfish, boned and skinned·

First make a stock of bones, horns and hooves of moose in three forty-gallon cauldrons. Meanwhile, fry fish in moose fat separately. Distribute fish equally to the three cauldrons and put six and two-thirds bushels of pine needles in each pot. Boil one hour or until tender. Strain out bones and needle pulp and discard. Place pared and sliced potatoes and moosemeat equally in cauldrons and simmer until tender. Serve in soup bowls with biscuits and fiddlehead salad and a fine rose wine.

MEDDYBEMPS BEANS
(Melange des legumes a la musique)

Pick over and select ten pounds each of yelloweye beans, soldier beans, pea beans, pinto beans, kidney beans, and Jacob's Cattle beans. Soak overnight.

Parboil the sixty pounds of beans in a very large saucepan. When skin blows back on a bean, shovel into a 250-quart cauldron. Heave in twenty-five pounds of salt pork and fifty pounds peeled onions. Add five gallons of molasses and five pounds of dry mustard and enough water to cover. Cook over moderate heat for three days, adding water at night.

Serves a small rural Maine household of four for supper.

As a kitchen medicine: At one time beans were held in high repute as a diuretic and cleanser of the kidneys and urethra of gravel and other concretions. A poultice of beans is good for removing facial moles and warts.

WELSH RATBIT
(Un petit rat Mainois)

Take a small Welshman and cover with a large copper washtub. Leave by the edge of a medium-sized coastal Maine dump. When the Welshman has obtained, by subterfuge and some cheddar cheese, three wharf rats, which must be at least fourteen and one-half centimeters thick, convey the Welshman and rats to your Kennebunk kitchen.

In a large frying pan, the Welshman moistens the cheddar and the rats with Narragansett beer, letting them blend over a medium temperature. Add some light soy sauce and a dozen chili peppers, stirring occasionally until thick and aromatic.

Have the Welshman pour the mixture over thick slices of Country Kitchen white toast. Brown the dish under the broiler of your Atlantic Queen. Serve with rice, fiddleheads and a good rose wine.

PRESSED CORMORANT
(Shag au sang)

First catch a cormorant by applying a goodly supply of birdlime about one of the rookeries. (Do not mind the smell.) Having caught several of these black birds, stun them with a rock until they are quite docile. Remove their innards and flay them with a sharp knife.

Find a flat piece of granite on which to place the still quivering bodies (insuring freshness) and slowly lower another equal-sized piece of granite on the birds, having first taken the precaution of ringing sponges about the stones to absorb the blood and other bodily juices.

Having wrung the blood and other juices into a small bowl, roast the bodies of the birds (better known as shags) on a low fire of driftwood for three hours. Cool, remove the bits of meat clinging to the roasted bodies, and combine with blood. Add a bottle of Silver Satin.

Chill the ingredients thoroughly until the liquids have slightly congealed. Pour over cold rice and serve with fiddleheads and a good rose wine.

UNFRIENDLIEST RESTAURANT IN MAINE

Now if you *love* nuclear power, Tat's Diner in downtown Wiscasset is just your cup of "hot" tea. But, if you don't, Tat's is more like a cup of hemlock, especially if you advertise your politics by hair longer than what men were wearing in 1955. Maine's vigorous nuclear-power-plant debate has divided the state, alas, even to the beaneries. Wiscasset is the most divided, being the site of the Maine Yankee plant.

Mark Melnicove

Tat's: Don't try to go to the bathroom either

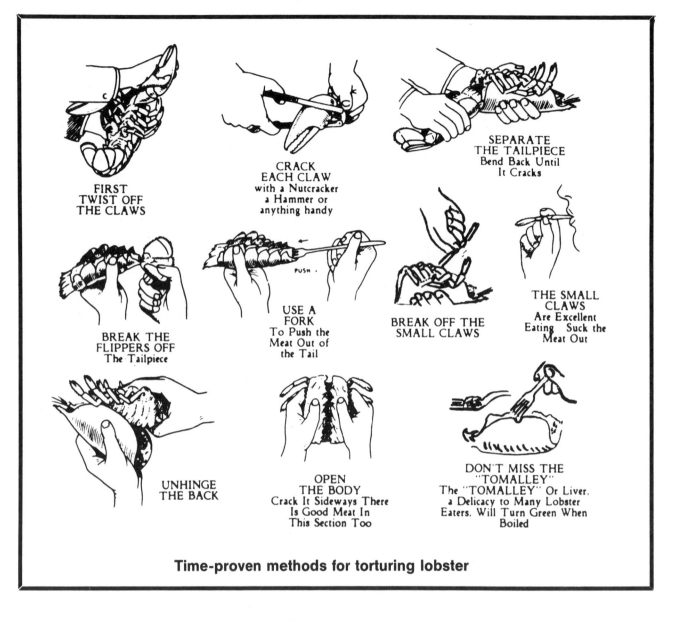

FIRST TWIST OFF THE CLAWS

CRACK EACH CLAW with a Nutcracker a Hammer or anything handy

SEPARATE THE TAILPIECE Bend Back Until It Cracks

BREAK THE FLIPPERS OFF The Tailpiece

USE A FORK To Push the Meat Out of the Tail

BREAK OFF THE SMALL CLAWS

THE SMALL CLAWS Are Excellent Eating   Suck the Meat Out

UNHINGE THE BACK

OPEN THE BODY Crack It Sideways There Is Good Meat In This Section Too

DON'T MISS THE "TOMALLEY" The "TOMALLEY" Or Liver. a Delicacy to Many Lobster Eaters, Will Turn Green When Boiled

Time-proven methods for torturing lobster

HOW TO TORTURE A LOBSTER

There are as many recipes for torturing the armor-plated crustacean *Homarus americanus* as there are people to think them up. The most popular recipe is to fill a pot with sea water and steam or boil the still-alive, kicking lobster for fifteen or so minutes.

Note the following variations to this recipe:
1) Left-wing terrorist lobsters should be left in an extra seven minutes to make sure they're not playing dead.
2) Fascist lobsters should be eaten raw so that they know what it's like to suffer.
3) Black nationalist lobsters (very rare in Vaca-

tionland) should be bleached before boiling so as not to prejudice the palate.

You can also bake lobsters and stew, pan fry or deep fry the lobster flesh. You can take a lighted cigarette and burn a hole in its genitals (if you can find them). The secret, no matter what recipe is used, is to never get caught by Amnesty International.

Why not stop in or call one of the many fine lobster pounds in Maine? They will be happy to give you instructions on the torture of lobsters. Many of their methods have been family secrets for generations.

How to Eat the Scenery

FOG SOUP

We have many foggy days in Maine. Fog is often called "pea soup." Unbeknownst to most, this fog can be eaten.

Take a sharp knife and go to where the fog is thickest, cut a large square of fog, bring back and place in a large kettle on the stove. Boil with ham hocks until soup is thick and flavorful. If you cannot afford ham hocks, you can substitute a large stone.

There are many poor people in Maine who do not have a proper diet. Some people who do have enough to eat think the poor people should move to states where they can get jobs more easily. Maine natives have recognized their predicament with their famous saying: "You can't eat the scenery!" Until now, eating the scenery has been thought impossible. But the authors of the *Guide* came across the following recipes which might suffice.

CEDAR SWAMP BROWSE

One of the most common ways poor folks supplement their diets is by shooting an illegal deer or two. This is not good. Some poachers wind up in jail. Why not skip the middleman and eat what the deer eat? Go to any large cedar grove and cut down several trees. Trim all the needles and bring them home. Steam as you would fiddleheads. You will find these very tasty greens supply you with enough energy to go out and get a job.

STONE IN
THE MOUTH

Go to any Maine beach. Find a small stone, wash it in salt water. Place in mouth. Suck until rock dissolves or hunger is satisfied. If flavor palls, soak again in salt water. One stone should last about three months. Caution: remove while sleeping.

Dave Witherell

Next best thing to eating the scenery: Friday morning at the Salvation Army in Augusta

4 Rich & Poor

Airplane Liz was a poor woman. She did nothing but collect wood to burn. She wore out six baby carriages collecting the wood. It was even rumored among the neighborhood children that she *ate* wood, she had so much of it. She had a little money, enough to pay for the twenty-five-cent tickets to the Saturday matinee where she sat down front with the kids watching the latest Lash LaRue. She kept her hat on in the movies, a beanie with a propeller which gave her her derogatory name. She collected so much wood that the neighbors declared it a fire hazard and the men from the city came and cleared the ground around her home. They promised her oil heat and put in a stove and said they would keep the tank full. The next day Airplane Liz was out collecting wood again. This time they didn't fool around but took her straight to Bangor State Hospital where she likely ended her days in some obscure corner.

On the other hand, Nelson Rockefeller was born rich in Seal Harbor. He didn't live there much, just on his vacations away from his homes in New York, Venezuela, etc. He collected wood, too. He collected strange wood carvings from a number of countries. He did not pile his wood around his house, but he put it in Central Park — in a museum there. Nelson did not go to the movies on Saturday afternoon; instead he helped run the government. Though he kept on collecting wood, no one put him in Bangor State Hospital or even Bellevue. Nelson died in an apartment in New York City with a beautiful, obscure girl. That is the difference between being rich and poor in Maine.

Let Them Eat Wood...

In 1983, the Legislature turned down a bill that would have raised the minimum wage from the national $3.35 an hour. But, according to unverified reports, the Governor signed another bill that encouraged anyone earning the minimum wage to eat wood. A new government charity program was set up to buy trimmings and edgings from lumber mills all over the state. These trimmings are to be ground into a fine powder that will be sold cheaply to add to flour or even to substitute for flour in bread, cakes, pies and doughnuts. Governor Brennan said that this contribution to human welfare worked well during the siege of Leningrad and should work well in Maine since we have the same climate as Russia.

"The condition of human life in that place is exceedingly wretched..."

Duc de la Rochefoucauld-Liancourt, on his 1795-96 trip to Maine

K.F. Mateychik

How Quaint: Maine's the Poorest State

A few years back the National Center for Economic Alternatives of Washington, D.C., did a study that subtracted the cost of living from the per-capita income of each of the states. Maine, which was forty-sixth in income, dropped to fiftieth when cost of living was figured in, bumping Mississippi for last place. The National Center blamed high food and energy prices for allowing Maine to win this distinction. This news, although it made banner headlines, was not well received by Maine's political leaders, who traditionally try to demonstrate that things are getting better and better under their rule. Maine even has a "state economist" whose job is to make rosy public predictions to make his boss, the governor, look good.

However, as recently as December, 1983, things did not appear to be getting any better. The federal Bureau of Labor Statistics released numbers showing that Maine workers were the lowest paid in the country except for Mississippi and South Dakota.

The news about Maine being the poorest state was hailed by the state's wealthy summer people because this meant that Maine's ramshackle quality of "quaintness," which is a direct function of per-capita income, was unlikely to be changed. Also, the minimum wage could continue to be paid to grateful, if irascible, handymen and maids. The liberal segment among the summer folk, however, were concerned that Maine's continuing poverty meant that more unsightly mobile homes would go on sprouting.

Mainers resigned to living here year-round reacted to the news by continuing to try to find ways to eat the scenery.

AN INTERVIEW WITH BUBBA AND ERLENE GEEK

UNCENSORED GUIDE INTERVIEWER: Well, Mr. Geek, how are you and the family today?

BUBBA: Finestkind, just call me Bubba, everybody does.

INTERVIEWER: Tell me, what is your occupation?

BUBBA: Oh, I job around, have a few traps, dig some clams, do a little carpenterin', a janitor job oncet a while, you know.

INTERVIEWER: Would you call yourself a handyman?

BUBBA: Waal, yes, you could call me that, I'm pretty handy.

ERLENE: Pretty handy at borryin' things.

BUBBA: Naow, Erlene you agreed that we wan't going to talk about that!

INTERVIEWER: What do you mean, borrowing things?

BUBBA: You ain't no cop, are you?

INTERVIEWER: No, I assure you this is for folklore purposes only.

BUBBA: Waal, borryin' means to take something that ain't yours. But we don't go in and clean out a place. If'n there was a set of four chairs we'd only take one. We'd only take half a tank of fuel oil or, if we was jackin' on someone else's land, we'd only shoot one or two.

ERLENE: Stealin' the Bible calls it. 'Thou shall not steal.'

BUBBA: You got to excuse Erlene, she got religion a couple of months ago and before that she borryed just as good as the rest of us.

ERLENE: I knowed I did but that was a sin and I been prayin' it out of my soul and you better do the same, Robert Geek!

INTERVIEWER: I didn't mean to cause trouble between you. Suppose we switch topics. How many traps do you fish?

BUBBA: She's been like this since she caught religion. I'll fix her later...I fish about seventy-five, a small string, but since I use a small boat I can get in closer to shore and I usually get a good haul.

ERLENE: 'Specially when you haul Tommy Plummer's or Nate Hall's traps.

BUBBA: I never!

ERLENE: I suppose you forgit the time Nate caught you at it and thrashed you within an inch of your life.

BUBBA: That was the once and only time, by Jesus.

ERLENE: I like to swear on a stack of Bibles that you haul a few side traps nearly every time you go out.

BUBBA: What about your beano, don't it say in the Bible, 'Thou shalt not gamble?'

ERLENE: No, it don't, but you know I'm tryin' to wean myself away from it. I don't claim to be totally redeemed, but I'm tryin'.

BUBBA: Huh! cut down to three nights from five! You still got a long way to go, sister!

INTERVIEWER: Where do you keep your traps, Mr. ...Bubba?

BRIDGES
TO SLEEP UNDER

EDWARD ARLINGTON ROBINSON BRIDGE, over Cobbosseecontee Stream, Gardiner. A bit breezy but near a diner and a pizza joint that you can smell.

LIMEROCK STREET BRIDGE, Rockland. A bit airy, too, but catches the smell from the dump.

BRUNSWICK-TOPSHAM CONNECTION. A good view of CMP's power dam on the Androscoggin. An occasional meal from the fishway is available.

MILLION-DOLLAR BRIDGE, Portland - South Portland. A warm (in summer) place to stay out of the wet if you don't have a million.

THE HIDEOUSLY HIGH SUSPENSION BRIDGE, Bucksport. This graceful bridge doesn't offer a lot of shelter, but it is close to Fort Knox, the name providing food for fantasies.

BUBBA AND ERLENE GEEK

BUBBA: Oh, I keep most around Spruce Island, pretty good fishin' except in the summer when the mosquito fleet is fishin'. Them little punks will set right on top of you — I'm afraid that I'm forced to cut a few.

INTERVIEWER: Don't they cut back?

BUBBA: Naw, they is all scairdt of me since the time I tied Billy Oliver to a trap and threw him over and didn't haul him up till I was damned good and ready — that scared 'em.

INTERVIEWER: Lobstering is a rough trade, it seems. I believe you said that you do some clamming also?

BUBBA: Yep, clammin' and wormin' — that pays pretty good if you stick to it regular.

ERLENE: Somethin' you never been known to do.

BUBBA: Look, woman, I had about all I want outa you. This here man is tryin' to understand the way I work and I was about to tell him that I got a bad back and can't dig all the time.

ERLENE: Especially the time we need food and I have to go to the town for grocery money.

BUBBA: You know what the doctor said, don't strain myself.

ERLENE: Now there's somethin' you never done.

INTERVIEWER: Well, Bubba, have you seen much change in the technology of the fishing industry?

BUBBA: Nothin' remarkable — I mean some of them fellas got real fancy-dancy radars and fish-scopes, but me I don't even have a hauler. No, I haul by hand and I just have a small outboard — used to row when I was a kid. I still use wooden traps except for a couple of wire ones I found.

ERLENE: Found with someone else's buoy and number...

INTERVIEWER: What about clamming?

BUBBA: Waal, that's the same as ever, bending and diggin, nothin' you can do about it.

ERLENE: Especially when it comes to closed flats.

BUBBA: Naow, I ain't been prosecuted but once for that and I got off on that one with a warnin'.

Typical TV antenna on Maine mobile home

TOP 12 OCCUPATIONS IN MAINE
1980

1. Sales clerks	13,603	8. Sales representatives (except insurance, real estate, stocks and bonds)	8,145
2. Janitors, porters, and cleaners	12,342		
3. Farm laborers	9,224	9. Cashiers	7,969
4. General clerks, office	9,127	10. Waiters or waitresses	7,967
5. Preschool and elementary school teachers	8,897	11. Secretaries	7,950
6. Farm owners and tenants	8,300	12. Nurse aides/ orderlies	7,748
7. Truck drivers	8,208		

Source: Maine Dept. of Labor

BUBBA AND ERLENE GEEK

ERLENE: That's because you had me and the whole seven kids and two of the neighbor's brats in court with you and you was wearin' that army uniform with your sharpshootin' medals.

BUBBA: I believe the lawyer said it was judged on the merits of the case.

ERLENE: How come you told the judge that you wouldn't be able to feed us all if'n you lost your license?

INTERVIEWER: Ah...how many hours a week would you say you put in on your lobstering and clamming and other fishing?

BUBBA: I'd say about forty-five.

ERLENE: You never! Why, I swear before God if you put in twenty it would be a miracle!

BUBBA: Erlene, I ain't gonna say this but once more, you shut up to my questions or I'll tell him how long it's been since you baked a pie!

INTERVIEWER: Now Bubba, how much do you socialize?

BUBBA: I'm not sure what you mean...socialism?

INTERVIEWER: How much do you go to church, dances, grange suppers, plays — that sort of thing?

ERLENE: Let me answer that, Mister Man.

BUBBA: You just keep shet up woman — he's interviewin' me.

INTERVIEWER: Well, either one of you would be fine.

BUBBA: I ain't darked a church door since I was twelve and got caught feeling up Lucy Tarbox in the belfry.

ERLENE: You sure as hell ain't goin' to darken Heaven's gate.

BUBBA: They used to have dances at the Grange Hall every Satiddy but now everybody stays home and watches Stacey's Country Jamboree. They only have a dance oncet a while at the Legion. We usually go now

that the kids is bigger. That's a good chance to do what do you call it — socialism?

INTERVIEWER: What kind of music do they play?

BUBBA: Waal, I don't pay too much attention, country and western, I guess, and an occasional Lady of the Lake.

ERLENE: He don't pay too much attention because he's always drunker 'n a skunk and I have to dance with my brother or some of the wimmen.

INTERVIEWER: Mrs. Geek, how much do you go to church?

ERLENE: Why, I expect about four times a week — including twice on Sunday. They's Sunday school and regular service Sunday mornin.' They's Sunday evening testimony time, Tuesday is the Golden Hour of Prayer and Praise and Friday evening is Ladies Missionary meetin.'

BUBBA: You see them Holy Rollers ain't satisfied to roll just once a week, they have to do it four or five nights as well.

INTERVIEWER: What denomination do you attend?

ERLENE: The First Church of Calvary Redeemed, Pentacostalist.

BUBBA: We always just called them Holy Rollers.

INTERVIEWER: Do you speak in tongues?

ERLENE: Why, yes we do...Just last week someone told me that I was speakin' German!

BUBBA: You was probably speaking junk and someone thought it was German.

ERLENE: It was German, I swear. Ellen Hodgkins told me and she spent two years there when her husband was in the Army.

BUBBA: I don't believe it, next thing you know you'll be speakin' English (laughs).

INTERVIEWER: What about plays and concerts,

Very quaint Maine homemade house

BUBBA AND ERLENE GEEK

do you ever go to any of them?

BUBBA: We went once to a Christmas play at school which our son Charley Pride Geek was in. Charley forgot his lines and wet his pants right there on the stage. He was awful cunnin.'

INTERVIEWER: How many children do you have?

ERLENE: We have seven and I hope to heaven we ain't havin' no more.

BUBBA: The oldest is Dick Curless Geek — he's seventeen and lives here with us with his girlfriend and their two kids. Then there's Johnny Cash Geek — he's in Boys Training down to South Portland. He set fire to the school house just like his uncle did. Then there's Kitty Wells Geek — she's thirteen and looks seventeen. She lives over to her boyfriend's house. Then there's Charley Pride Geek, he's twelve and lives with us. Anne Murray Geek is ten and she lives here, too. The two youngest, Loretta Lynn Geek and Waylon Jennings Geek, are living on the state.

INTERVIEWER: What do you mean, living on the state?

BUBBA: Waal, one of these goddamned social workers come out one time and said we was neglectin' 'em and that they had to be put in foster homes. I can't understand it, we didn't treat them no different from the others.

ERLENE: The shame of it — now that I go to church reglar. I'm hopin' to get 'em back for they was my little darlins and I only git to see 'em once a month — that ain't right, not for kith and kin.

INTERVIEWER: I noticed a number of cars in the yard — how many do you own?

BUBBA: Waal, that's a good question...we got six in the yard but all but two of 'em are junkers. I mostly drive the '78 Ford pickup and Erlene drives the convertible — that is, when it's runnin'.

INTERVIEWER: Why do you keep so many cars that don't work?

BUBBA: Oh, I don't know, they just seem to accumulate. Gives the kids something to play in and I kinda like their looks in the yard.

ERLENE: What he means, he's too cheap to get them hauled off.

BUBBA: I'm gonna haul off and do somethin' if you don't watch it, woman.

INTERVIEWER: Do you get taxed on them?

BUBBA: Naw, jist the two that's workin'. They tried to get me with personal property for 'em but I said I wouldn't pay and showed 'em to the door and they ain't said nothin' since. Goddamn zonin' board trying to get me to clean up but I'm grandfathered in — keep tellin' 'em my grandfather gave 'em to me (laughs).

ERLENE: I jist don't know — I try to pretty up the yard with flowers and painted white rocks and flamingoes and he just messes it up with this and that. If'n it ain't another car, it's a pile of slabs or a bunch of wore-out traps. Can't fix up anything around here without it gettin' ruint.

BUBBA: I wish you'd tend to your cooking more than the yard and we wouldn't have so many ruint

Guy Gannett Newspapers

"Miss Dumpy," Kennebunkport's 1983 dump queen

BUBBA AND ERLENE GEEK

meals...I shoulda married Evie Trott, I hear she's a right hand at baking pie.

ERLENE: But you didn't get her pregnant, did you, huh, Robert Geek?

INTERVIEWER: Ah...how did you two meet?

ERLENE: He was always after me 'cause I had the biggest tits in town.

BUBBA: I always admired her and one day she came down to the bait house to bait up for her daddy and I saw her and jist went over and kissed her. Soon enough she was knocked up and we had to git married. She was what you called well built.

ERLENE: I'm still well built but I've jist expanded all around.

INTERVIEWER: Where did you live when you first got married?

BUBBA: We lived with my daddy and ma but after a couple of years things got rather tight, for they had another kid, so we moved into that house back there behind the trailer (points out the window to a small tar-paper shack).

INTERVIEWER: When did you get this trailer?

BUBBA: It was in ' 72. This guy had the trailer and he had a fire in it and was going to junk it so I asked him if'n I could haul it away and he said he would give me twenty-five dollars if I did. I brought it here and fixed it up. All's took was a few sheets of paneling and it was good as new.

ERLENE: Well, not quite. It were three years before we got electricity and we're still using our old outhouse, and we've got to git our water from the spring down the road and we have to be chary with it.

INTERVIEWER: I notice you have two refrige-

Ode to the Dump

The governmentally enforced closing of many dumps in Maine is a great tragedy. Where else can people in small towns get together? Think of the affairs that started when someone admired the way someone else neatly packed his or her garbage. The dump was a center of political activity where local people could discuss the affairs of the town in the fresh, clean air. It was the place where people gathered on a Saturday morning to shoot rats. What better location could there be for community development? Many is the politician who has been elected by passing out cards at the dump where everyone was grateful for something to take home, feeling perhaps they had left too much behind.

And the smell. Think of how grateful everyone was that they didn't have to live at the dump! It was a blessing to know that despite the messiness of the home front it was not quite as bad as the dump. The dump was also a center of education. From the very earliest days in a child's life, one knew that eventually everything broke and decayed and was thrown out — the impermanence of life itself was shown to the little toddlers playing in the mud at the dump.

Think of the town history that will be lost. Archeologists in the future will think most of the Maine small towns died out in the early nineteen-eighties — the years the garbage stopped. If it is shipped to a nearby town and burned to make power, no one will know how we lived. Does that matter, you ask? Of course. How will the world know you were a great lover without reading all your old love letters? How will they know when you went on a diet? How will they know you gave to UNICEF? Many questions that historians and social scientists ask about the past depends upon garbage. Why the whole of Colonial Williamsburg is built on garbage research! No, absolute cleanliness is not all! The past is prologue and much of that prologue lies in the local dump.

BUBBA AND ERLENE GEEK

rators.

BUBBA: One of 'em is a freezer — keep that full of deer and moosemeat.

ERLENE: Yeah, Bubba earned his sharpshootin' medal in the army for the good reason that he'd been shootin' out of season for years.

BUBBA: Yep! Once in July I even skun a deer on the warden's front lawn and he never found out who did it (laughs).

INTERVIEWER: Aren't you worried about being caught?

BUBBA: Naw, I got a CB and a scanner in my truck and in the house, too. They's a bunch of us fellas that cooperate and we can tell where John Law is most of the time — we don't worry none about them. If'n anybody gits caught it's jist because he was foolish and didn't have someone along to give warnin'.

INTERVIEWER: Do you have a garden?

BUBBA: I trained Charlie to find things and he keeps us in veggies most of the summer. He's pretty good jist with his bicycle and lookin' 'round — he only got shot at once. I call him the Raccoon 'cause people think that's what got in their gardens!

ERLENE: This here has got to stop! Charley is going to be just like you and he might end up where his brother is in that awful place down to South Portland.

BUBBA: Don't you worry about Charley. If'n he sticks to the way I told him he'll never get caught — he's got a mind just like a raccoon!

ERLENE: Yeah, well I wish he would wash his hands as often as a coon does, he's the dirtiest boy in three counties.

BUBBA: Once I get water piped in and I find a water heater we can have showers every day.

ERLENE: If you took half your beer money and put it in a well we'd have been washing long ago.

INTERVIEWER: Do you mind if I ask what brand you drink?

BUBBA: Waal, I started out on Nastygansett 'cause they used to sponsor the Red Sox games, but since they stopped I switched to Bud and it seems a little better.

INTERVIEWER: How many do you average a day?

BUBBA: Oh, three or four in the evenin' when I'm watching TV.

ERLENE: By the Jerusalem, Bubba, you know they's hardly a day when you don't drink two sixpacks and sixteen ouncers at that. Look at the gut on you!

BUBBA: Waal, look at the gut on you — comes from eatin' all them chocolate-covered cherries. I may have a six pack or so but no more. You want this guy here to think I'm a candidate for Alkies Anonymous?

ERLENE: Waal, I'm sure it wouldn't do you no harm. They's some nice people that belongs to it and they learn to be more respectful of themselves and other people.

BUBBA: Lissen, Mrs. Bubba, I guess I can be respectful when I want to be. I don't need the organized company of no alkies — I can meet enough of them at the Legion and other places.

ERLENE: You surely do that. Why your borrying club is all a bunch of drunks anyway.

INTERVIEWER: What's your borrowing club?

BUBBA: Oh, just a bunch of fellas I hang around with. We call ourselves the Black Snakes and we all have this snake tattooed on our arm.

INTERVIEWER: Where do you meet?

BUBBA: Oh, we have a clubhouse back in the woods, jist for git-togethers you understand. Do a little coon hunting and oncet a while we go up north to hunt bear — that's where I got that rug over there.

ERLENE: Mostly they get together to go out borrying.

BUBBA: Yep, we make a little on the side helping out pickers — pays out our expenses and the bar tab.

INTERVIEWER: What are pickers?

BUBBA: Antique pickers. A dealer gives him an order for a customer, he comes to us and we find what he wants.

ERLENE: By stealin'!

BUBBA: We jist borry here and there. Like I said, we never clean out a place — we spread the trade around pretty good.

THE WELL-DRESSED MAINEIAC

BUBBA:
white cotton socks under wool red socks
long underwear all year 'round
hip boots folded below the knee
green Dickies pants
green Dickies shirt
green Dickies hat when working,
    baseball cap when dressed up
belt with a Marine Corps buckle
green and black plaid jacket, winter and
    summer
Marlboro cigarettes

ERLENE:
white socks
moccasins
pink bra, panties and girdle in summer,
    long underwear in winter
plastic-fabric blouse
green knit polyester pantsuit
acryllic sweater

BUBBA AND ERLENE GEEK

INTERVIEWER: Do you ever get caught?

BUBBA: Nope, we keep a good watch on John Law, come in by boat to these places on the water and keep our scanners on — we're pretty careful.

INTERVIEWER: Don't you ever feel...bad about stealing things from others?

BUBBA: Naw. We only hit the places where they got more than is good for 'em. We're just simplifyin' their lives for 'em.

ERLENE: We've had the sheriff nosing around here for some time, so it's probably jist a matter of time afore he catches up with you.

BUBBA: I ain't worrit. That bastard will never catch us...he ain't gonna get re-elected anyway.

INTERVIEWER: That brings up another subject — what political party do you belong to?

BUBBA: I am an Independent.

ERLENE: You ain't never been rigistered, you ain't no independent! You ain't never even voted!

BUBBA: That's what I mean, I am independent of all political parties and votin'.

An Interview with Priscilla and Parkhurst Volvo

UNCENSORED GUIDE INTERVIEWER: Did you build this home yourselves?

PARK: We designed it and helped the builders. I took the Shelter Institute course.

MAINE MEDIA PREFERENCES

THE GEEKS:

> **Paul Harvey News**
> **Bangor Daily News**
> **Saturday Edition (for comics)**
> **Midnight**
> **National Enquirer**
> **Hustler**
> **Country and western radio**
> **Stacey's Country Jamboree**
> **All Star Wrestling**

THE VOLVOS:

> **Radio Reader**
> **The rest of public radio**
> **The rest of public television**
> **Maine Times (for personals)**
> **New York Sunday Times**
> **Gourmet**
> **Smithsonian**
> **Architectural Digest**
> **Antiques**
> **Boston Globe Sunday Edition (for comics)**
> **National Review**
> **Audubon Magazine**
> **New Yorker (for cartoons)**
> **The Atlantic Monthly**
> **Forbes**

PRIS: And I took the Cornerstones course. We didn't want to miss anything.

INTERVIEWER: Is this what's called a postindustrial home?

PARK: Yes, in that most of the beams were rescued from decaying barns.

PRIS: No, in that everything else came from the housing industry.

INTERVIEWER: How do you heat it?

PARK: Well, it's a solar envelope home with a Russian fireplace.

PRIS: We also have backup electric heat and an oil furnace.

PARK: Yes, we were quite cold in the old cape we restored when we first moved to Maine, so we decided to be ready for every eventuality.

INTERVIEWER: You certainly have a nice view here. What is that river?

PARK: Oh, that's the Sheepscot.

PRIS: I'm afraid only four hundred feet of it is ours, even though we have thirteen acres. You know how expensive waterfront property is these days.

PARK: I'm afraid we got scalped on this land. We paid well over thirty thousand dollars for it.

PRIS: Yes, if we hadn't made such a profit on our cape I don't know if we could have afforded it.

INTERVIEWER: Where do you work?

PARK: I have a law office in Wiscasset and I spend one day a week in Portland.

PRIS: I do mostly volunteer work at Miles Memorial Hospital in Damariscotta and at the library there. I have a little trust fund, and Daddy always wanted me to help other people.

INTERVIEWER: Where did you go to college?

PRIS: I have a B.A. in English from Bennington and

Priscilla and Parkhurst Volvo

an M.S.W. in social work from Smith.

PARK: Amherst and Harvard Law...and the U.S. Navy.

INTERVIEWER: Mrs. Volvo, did you ever practice social work?

PRIS: I did in Roxbury for almost a year in a day-care center, but when I met Parkie I stopped.

PARK: The place was a shambles and I kept telling her it was dangerous.

INTERVIEWER: Do you have children?

PRIS: We have Paul who is seventeen and Pamela who is twelve.

INTERVIEWER: Do they go to local schools?

PRIS: Oh, no! Heavens, they're dreadful!

PARK: Paul is a senior at Exeter and Pamela goes to the Waynflete School in Portland.

INTERVIEWER: Isn't that expensive?

PRIS: Well, Daddy left them a little trust fund each and it can be used for their education. We feel the results will be worth it.

INTERVIEWER: Don't you think there is some danger they will become some sort of elite — out of touch with common men and women?

PARK: Oh, no, we don't worry about that — look how we turned out!

PRIS: We send the kids to Maine camps in the summer and they get along well with everyone and they have local friends. Once Paul brought home a boy who goes to Wiscasset High School.

INTERVIEWER: How do you get along with your neighbors?

PARK: On one side, fine, the man is a librarian at Bowdoin and we can talk with him, but on the other side is the most disgusting family.

INTERVIEWER: What do you mean?

PRIS: Well, they're dirty in both mind and body. *And* they own 1,200 feet on the river.

INTERVIEWER: Are they rich?

PARK: I should say not, they're always behind in their taxes but they claim to have inherited the land, though I can't see why anyone in his right mind would have left them anything.

PRIS: At last count there were seven cars in their yard that didn't work and several that just barely go.

PARK: They intimidate our guests when they drive by.

PRIS: Yes, and call me Mrs. Rich Bitch!

INTERVIEWER: Can't you complain to the police?

PRIS: Oh, we've tried, but the sheriff seems to be some sort of relative and he says they don't mean any serious harm, they're just high spirited.

Priscilla and Parkhurst Volvo

PARK: Probably high spirited from all the spirits they indulge in and all the pot they grow in their cornfield.
PRIS: Well, you should never have bought anything from them and they wouldn't have anything on us!
PARK: But what could we do, we were having a party and I couldn't get any from my usual source?
PRIS: We'll be paying for that party for a long time.
PARK: Damn it Priscilla, we had to have the stuff!
INTERVIEWER: Ah...what kind of law do you practice, Mr. Volvo?
PARK: Well, I specialize in admiralty law, but with the decline of the American shipping establishment, a crying shame really, I don't have many cases. I only spend a day a week working in Portland and two days a week in Wiscasset doing divorces and deed work. Two days a week I take sculpture courses at the Portland School of Art.
INTERVIEWER: So you're an artist as well?
PARK: Not yet, maybe someday...but we have toyed with the idea of setting up a gallery in Wiscasset.
PRIS: I'd love to run it — we'd have good art — not that usual stuff that populates these coastal galleries.
PARK: Yes, most of it is dreadful — not even art really.
INTERVIEWER: Have you sold any of your sculptures?

**Exciting Activities to Do in Maine
in the Wintertime**

> *"They wish to sell because they have done too little work around them to have placed their affections there."*
>
> Tallyrand, 1700s,
> on Maine people's propensity to sell land

PARK: Why, I've given away several fairly large pieces to schools.
INTERVIEWER: Do you think of giving up law for the world of art permanently?
PARK: I wouldn't mind, but the terms of my trust fund are that I maintain my status as an admiralty lawyer. The family made its money in shipping and Dad wanted us to continue contact with it...It's the American thing to do, he always said.
PRIS: We do everything American except for French bread.
PARK: And clothing. I can't seem to get a decent fit here so every three years or so we travel to London for our tailoring.
PRIS: But, besides that, we buy American. Except for our cars.
INTERVIEWER: What do you have for cars?
PARK: Why Volvos, of course. Pris has a station wagon, I have a sedan turbo and Paul has a nicely re-stored P-1800.
INTERVIEWER: How did you get your rather unusual name?
PARK: Well, Dad admired their engineering and had our name changed.
PRIS: And it's in his trust fund that he must drive Volvos.
INTERVIEWER: How unusual.
PARK: Well, they are the safest car built.
INTERVIEWER: I noted that you have a Volvo pickup with a plow attached. Isn't that a bit unusual?
PARK: We're pretty proud of that. Paul and I built it from our '78 wagon that was getting on in mileage. The plow is mostly for effect. It won't handle anything heavy, so we are plowed out by a local fellow, but this pickup causes a sensation wherever we go.

MAINE MILLIONAIRES

Maine, by some accounts, is the poorest state in the Union. Notwithstanding that, however, it is second only to Idaho in per-capita millionaires — with 8,830 of them, according to a 1979 report. These are not the ostentatious millionaires of Bar Harbor of former times, but those tucked into neat little capes on the road to Bristol. Most have retired with their money from away, for the opportunity to earn a million here in poor old Maine is very rare.

You're Not Welcome in Winslow Homer Land (But Some Go Anyway)

Prout's Neck in Scarborough, south of Portland, is the locale of Winslow Homer's studio and of many of his most famous paintings. Maybe you have thought of visiting the studio and the shore he so often painted, but perhaps you never got beyond this sign:

Winslow Homer Road

Positively No Passing
PRIVATE WAY

For members
and their guests only

As described by the *Maine Times*, Prout's Neck is one of the most exclusive summer colonies on the Maine coast, which is pretty exclusive in a general sense because very little of it is not privately owned. Prout's Neck has its own private police force, the Prouts Neck Beach Association, the Prouts Neck Yacht Club, and the Prouts Neck Country Club with an eighteen-hole golf course and fourteen tennis courts. Among its shingle-and-stone "cottages" are many No Parking and No Trespassing signs — designed to keep out undesirables such as Democrats, tourists and Maine year-round residents. There is even a guard posted on the golf course to keep the public from strolling onto the fairways from the nearby beaches. The book *Old Prouts Neck* describes the community: "Here an attempt was made to plant a settlement upon the ancient lines of pure aristocracy and kingly authority, united with the religious ideals of the Church of England."

However, people still go down Winslow Homer Road to visit Homer's studio, where the owners kindly make it available to the public.

FREEPORT —
A TRADE ZONE FOR THE RICH

L.L. Bean's creates a great pull to tourists coming up I-95. Some of these people drive Mercedes, Cadillacs, BMW's, Volvos, Saabs. It is natural that other stores would like to cash in on this tony trade. So now we have many shops in Freeport that can suit this sort of customer. Of course, the ordinary Maine shopper can't even look in the window without a heart attack. Most Maineiacs still think that the $40-50 that L.L. charges for his cheapest boots is high. They simply don't

believe a handsewn pair of loafers from Cole Hahn for $99.

It is rumored that the town fathers and mothers of Freeport may soon pass an ordinance prohibiting Maine natives on the streets between 8 a.m. to 8 p.m. It is also rumored that dozens of young men and women from New Jersey have been hired to wear L.L. Bean clothing and impersonate Maine people during these hours.

Ayuh — The Potato Pickin' Song
(to the tune of "Dayo-the Banana Boat Song")

AYUH, I Said Ayuh!
Gettin' Dark and I want to go home.
AYUH! I Said Ayuh, ayuh, ayuh!
Gettin' dark and I want to go home.

> Come Mister Digger Man count up my potatoes.
> *Gettin' dark and I want to go home.*
> Come Mr. Digger Man count up my potatoes.
> *Gettin' dark and I want to go home.*
> One potato two potato three potato four.
> *Gettin' dark and I want to go home.*
> Five potato six potato seven potato more.
> *Gettin' dark and I want to go home.*

(Repeat chorus)

> Live in a trailer at the edge of the spud field.
> *Gettin' dark and I want to go home.*
> All the wallpaper is made out of spud peels.
> *Gettin' dark and I want to go home.*
> Bake stuff, french fry, boiled up or mash.
> *Gettin' dark and I want to go home.*
> Augratin, all rotten, scallop or hash.
> *Gettin' dark and I want to go home.*

(Repeat chorus)

Words by Stephen Bither and Jere DeWaters. ©1983 Wicked Good Music.

5 *Crime*

One of the safest places to be in Maine theoretically is the town of Limestone, which in 1982 had a crime rate of 8.26 crimes per thousand people, the lowest in the state except for Van Buren, which discontinued its police force in March of 1982. Limestone had no murders, no rapes, no robberies, only one aggravated assault, only twenty-three burglaries, forty-five larcenies and three motor vehicle thefts in a population of 8,719.

Of course there is one slight problem with living in Limestone — it is one of the prime nuclear targets in the world, being a major if outdated SAC base. So if you want to get away from crime, there is the place to get away from it. At some risk to your future.

Nearly anywhere in rural Maine in January is safe if one can stand the cabin fever — most small towns have little crime except for an occasional killing every few years *because* of cabin fever, plus burglaries and assaults.

If you want excitement, what little there is of it in the state, you must go to Portland — but you will pay for it. The 1983 crime rate per thousand is 103.75, or more than ten times Limestone's. It had five murders, twenty-two rapes, ninety-five robberies, 311 assaults, 1,602 burglaries, 3,871 larcenies, 382 motor vehicle thefts, and 100 cases of arson. You have the highest rate, naturally enough, in the biggest city. And now probably Portland, too, is a nuclear target with its new BIW shipyard.

Only eight states, all very rural except Pennsylvania, have crime rates lower than Maine's. Vermont's is the lowest. Mississippi's total crime rate is lower, but you are seven times more likely to be murdered in Mississippi than in Maine.

What Cabin Fever Leads to

THE CASE OF TWO MURDERERS

Probably the most famous murder case in Maine history is that of Paul Dwyer and Francis Carroll. In October of 1937, Paul Dwyer was discovered sleeping in a small town in New Jersey in a car registered in Maine. On investigating, the local police found two bodies in the car — that of Dr. Littlefield and his wife, residents of South Paris, Maine. Dwyer gave several confessions which varied considerably. He was arrested, taken back to South Paris and tried in December. Soon after the trial began, he confessed, pleaded guilty, and was sent to prison.

Just before he left the county jail, he told one of the deputies that the real killer was one Francis Carroll, a deputy sheriff and father of Dwyer's girlfriend Barbara. Carroll, he said, had been committing incest with Barbara, and he killed the doctor when he threatened to expose him. Much was made of the fact that Dwyer was so small and thin that he supposedly could not have moved the bodies to the doctor's car. Dwyer said that Carroll had also killed the doctor's wife.

In June of 1938 the grand jury met to consider indicting Carroll for incest and ended up indicting him for murder. A twelve-day trial followed in August and Carroll was found guilty of the murder of the doctor. No one was tried for his wife's murder, Dwyer was not released, and so two men were serving time for the same murder.

About a dozen years later Carroll was released on a writ of habeus corpus and later died of cancer...Dwyer was released in 1961 after serving over twenty years. He still lives in Maine.

INTERVIEW WITH A TYPICAL MAINE CRIMINAL

This is an interview with Howland (Howlin') Geek conducted at the Maine State Prison in Thomaston.

UNCENSORED GUIDE INTERVIEWER: Now, Mr. Geek, how long are you in for?

GEEK: Call me Howlin', everybody does.

INTERVIEWER: All right, Howlin', how long are you in for?

GEEK: Six years, minus my good time.

INTERVIEWER: Is this your first sentence?

GEEK: Hell no! I been in Boys Training, Windham, Augusta State, Bangor State and Togus....The only place I ain't been in is up to Skowhegan with the ladies, but that's closed now.

INTERVIEWER: A life of crime, eh?

GEEK: Crime and crazy. Not much of a life.

INTERVIEWER: Which do you think you are, a criminal, or mentally ill?

GEEK: Why mental, of course, I wouldn't'a done them things otherwise.

INTERVIEWER: How come you're here then, in prison instead of Augusta or Togus?

GEEK: Well the jury was rigged, that's all I can say.

INTERVIEWER: What were you convicted of?

GEEK: Enterin'

INTERVIEWER: Do you mean "Breaking and Entering" ?

GEEK: There weren't no "breakin' " about it, the damned place was unlocked.

INTERVIEWER: What were you doing in the house you entered then?

GEEK: Just gettin' warm — I'd been out huntin' coot and dark come on sudden and it was jeezly cold and I jist went ashore and went in the first place I come to to get warmed up.

INTERVIEWER: But the court records say you had two paintings and a camera in your boat and that you were pulling down the shore when the deputy sheriff caught you.

GEEK: Oh, them — I was just gonna borry them for my camp for a month or so — pretty it up a little, then take 'em back after Christmas.

INTERVIEWER: What were the paintings you took?

GEEK: Why, I thought they was original Andy's but it turned out they was just copies — the two of 'em not worth over a hundred.

INTERVIEWER: What do you mean, "Andys" ?

GEEK: Where you been, fella? Andy's are anything by Andy Wyeth. He paints a lot of people around here and gives some of 'em away. It always pays to be on the lookout for 'em.

INTERVIEWER: So you did steal them?

GEEK: Well the DA convinced the jury of that.

INTERVIEWER: You said you were mentally ill. Did you plead insanity?

GEEK: Oh! I tried to, but they wouldn't have none of it. You see I done similar before.

INTERVIEWER: How did it all start out?

CRIME CLOCK

In the Maine State Police headquarters in Augusta, there is a special clock installed by order of the legislature that loses only two seconds in ten thousand years. This clock has a series of special attachments that make sounds to remind the cops how much is going on around them while they sit there playing Parcheesi:

Every 15 days a shotgun goes off indicating that a murder has taken place.

Every 58 hours, a woman's voice cries "Help! Help! Rape!"

Every 25 hours, 28 minutes and 54 seconds a gruff male voice says: "Stick 'em up!"

Every 16 hours, 26 minutes, 7 seconds there is the sound of a match lighting up.

Every six hours, 36 minutes and 58 seconds comes the sound of a punch hitting a jaw.

Every 4 hours, 3 minutes and 47 seconds a hot-wired car starts up.

Every 44 minutes, 21 seconds, the sound of breaking glass indicates a burglary.

And, finally, every 18 minutes, 52 seconds, the sound of a can of soup being slid into a trench coat pocket tells of another larceny.

As you can see, compared to, say, Los Angeles, this is pretty slow-moving activity.

But this special clock is the conscience of the police in Maine and gives them pause throughout the days and weeks and months. They think about how to stop this number of crimes from happening as they go on playing Parcheesi.

GEEK: My first time was when I was eleven. They wouldn't let me in the Boy Scouts down home to Hancock County, so I burned down some tents out in back of the school that they had.

INTERVIEWER: What happened to you for that?

GEEK: I got three years in Boys Training.

INTERVIEWER: For burning a couple of tents?

GEEK: Waal, you see the fire got loose and burnt down the school. It was jist one of those one-room jobbers, but it was the only town school they had at the time. The way I figure it I did them a good turn. They collected the insurance and built a nice new place. The way I figure it they shouldda named it after me.

INTERVIEWER: Let's get back to the Boys Training Center — how was that?

GEEK: It was the pits, but that's where I learned insanity.

INTERVIEWER: What do you mean — learned insanity?

GEEK: Waal, we always had these psychologists and social workers pryin' around about how we was thinking and pretty soon I learned how to answer 'em so's that they would take pity on me and I got out a year early. It's been workin' for me ever since, at least off and on.

INTERVIEWER: Where was the next place you were incarcerated?

GEEK: As you might expect, since I learned insanity, it was up to Bangor State Hospital. That place was really a can o' worms, but there was girls there, so it was better than BT, and after you learned to fake taking your medicine it was fairly tolerable. It was easy to play insanity too, cause all the docs up there was foreigners. I swear they couldn't understand a damn word I said. I

The "Bunny" Zahn Story

On Nov. 13, 1982, a seventy-seven-foot vessel began unloading thirty tons of Colombian marijuana in forty-pound bales on Bernie "Bunny" Zahn's lobster dock in Bremen. Nothing unusual here, except for the size of the ship. This sort of thing goes on all the time on the Maine coast. What was unusual were the cops in the woods, tipped off by an informer, who spoiled the operation by arresting twenty-four men including Bernie, 66, the scandal-familiar former head of the Maine Liquor Commission. He had been in his adjacent house at the time of the raid, and police had observed his house lights flicking on and off as the freighter approached the dock. The cops took this as a signal.

Bernie's arrest was a little embarrassing to some Maine political figures: his daughter, State Senator Charlotte Sewall, and his son-in-law, Loyall Sewall, who runs the Republican Party in Maine as its chairman. So it came as a relief to them when U.S. Attorney Richard Cohen, who owes his job to Republican patronage, presented evidence to the federal grand jury that resulted in the indictment of twenty-three of the twenty-four men — all but Bunny Zahn.

Zahn's complaint was dismissed while ten Maine clamdiggers and fishermen and eight bewildered Colombians marched off to jail. Unlike Bernie, many of these people had no records. When he had been chairman of the Liquor Commission in 1952 he had resigned during an investigation into whether he had tried to exert political pressure in connection with a liquor license. The *Portland Press Herald* reported that he "was subsequently indicted and fined $500." He later was charged with having been part of a bribery-conspiracy scheme while he was commission chairman, but was found not guilty of this, the paper said.

Guy Gannett Newspapers

Bernie "Bunny" Zahn in handcuffs

After Bernie got off, an informer in the marijuana operation testified in court that arrangements for the smuggling had been made with Zahn. One of the defense attorneys in the case told the newspapers that "there was a feeling [among defense attorneys] that Zahn's case wasn't presented to the grand jury quite as vigorously as some of the others."

Incidentally, the name of the vessel involved was the "Indomable." This is conclusive evidence that dope smoking destroys the ability to spell words properly.

sure couldn't understand what they said.

INTERVIEWER: Why were you put there in the first place?

GEEK: I was foolin' around with a girl.

INTERVIEWER: That isn't madness.

GEEK: But she was only twelve.

INTERVIEWER: How old were you?

GEEK: I was twenty-three.

INTERVIEWER: What happened?

GEEK: She got pregnant.

INTERVIEWER: That's not good.

GEEK: 'Specially since she was my sister's kid.

INTERVIEWER: I thought that would put you in prison.

GEEK: I plea-bargained my way into the nuthouse — never did regret it. After I got used to the place we had some good parties.

INTERVIEWER: You mentioned earlier that you had been in Togus. I thought that was for veterans only.

GEEK: I am a veteran.

INTERVIEWER: How did you get in, with your record?

GEEK: During the Nam period, they'd take anything that could walk and carry an M-16.

INTERVIEWER: How long were you in Viet Nam?

GEEK: Oh! I never made it that far. Some guy who had just come back told me what it was like, and I said to myself, that's crazy! I thought of going AWOL, but instead I pleaded insanity and got out in four months. I get a nice little pension for that —$195 per month with no taxes and all the free treatment I want. Pretty rich, huh?

INTERVIEWER: I'm confused now. Don't you always go to Togus? How do you get into Augusta?

GEEK: Sometimes I lie and tell I ain't a veteran. They's hardly any women at Togus.

INTERVIEWER: Now you're in prison.

GEEK: Yep, it's better than the ward for the criminally insane up to Augusta. Some of them birds are crazy!!! One guy tried to bite my ear off — look here, they's still scars.

INTERVIEWER: Yes, very interesting.

GEEK: It used to be a pretty good life here till the crackdown.

INTERVIEWER: What do you mean?

GEEK: Oh, my friend Charlie ran the place from his cell, and if you were one of his buddies you got everything you wanted 'ceptin' maybe women.

INTERVIEWER: What happened?

GEEK: Governor Brennan came here and took it all away — my TV, stereo, frigerator, my *Penthouses* — said they was unauthorized material. Christ, I paid for 'em, a man ought to be able to keep what he pays for...When I get out of here I'm going back to Augusta and get me a comfortable apartment — no more stealin' for me, and no more coot shootin' if you get my meanin'.

INTERVIEWER: You're going to live straight?

GEEK: Yes, I think I will, no more partying, no more selling dope, and for goddam sure no more digging clams — it was gittin' to my back. I'll be a good little boy and live off my pension and SSI.

INTERVIEWER: Do you feel that life has cheated you somehow?

GEEK: Hell, No! I cheated it. I've hardly done a day's work in my life — see here, I'm fat. That mean's I'm well fed. I've had more women than you can shake a stick at, and booze and drugs. That's what counts in life, ain't it? That's all any man needs.

INTERVIEWER: What if everybody lived like that?

GEEK: What if they did? They'd be a hell of a lot happier.

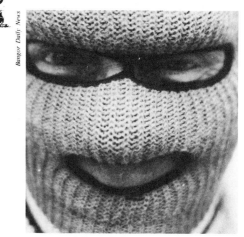

Typical Maine crime attire

Bangor Daily News

Typical coastal scene; bales of dope in the foreground

GREAT DRUG-SMUGGLING DEFENSES

Drug smuggling on Maine's complex coast has spawned a number of innovative legal defenses when the alleged smugglers are charged with what has become a commonplace crime.

The Religious Defense was tried by members of the Ethiopian Zion Coptic Church in federal court in Portland. Judge Edward Gignoux disallowed the defense before the trial, saying if marijuana were allowed for religious purposes "marijuana laws would be meaningless and enforcement impossible."

This did not prevent members of the church from trying to convince the jury that mary jane was part of their sacred rites. They claimed they needed two ounces to one pound each to carry on their prayer sessions held thrice daily. When the prosecution pointed out that 1,263 bales of the stuff were taken from the ship *Jubilee* in the 1980 arrest, High Priest Reilly, brought from federal prison in Miami where he is serving a fifteen-year marijuana conspiracy sentence, said marijuana is sometimes used to stimulate the appetite of livestock raised by the church members for food, and to calm animals before they are slaughtered.

The jury put religious arguments aside and convicted them on Dec. 17, 1982, of possession and conspiracy charges. Sixteen people were sentenced to five to nine years.

The Viet Nam War Syndrome was tried as a defense by a hapless veteran. Michael J. Tindall of Plainsboro, New Jersey, was arrested at Moxie Cove in Round Pond in 1976. He claimed the stresses of the war not only drove him to partake of pot and other drugs but to import them. But Maine juries are about as sympathetic as Marine Corps DIs. He began serving two years in March, 1983.

The case which caused the greatest interest in Maine was the Literary Defense of Richard Stratton, a friend of Norman Mailer, who testified at his trial. Stratton claimed his participation was only to research a novel. However, Maine juries aren't filled with literary types. He was convicted in April, 1983, to serve fifteen years.

Statue of Count Dracula, Bangor. In the foreground, some admirers

Members of the Ethiopian Zion Coptic Church outside the federal courthouse in Portland

ROGUE'S GALLERY
Maine Has 2 on FBI "Most Wanted" List

It's a small state, but sometimes our folks do things in a big way. For example, the FBI has made a big deal over the alleged bank robberies, murder, terrorism and bombings of the Levasseur Gang, which was hatched in little ol' Portland, Maine. The group began life in the midseventies in acts of

Ray Luc Levasseur

protest to our Greedy Capitalist Exploitative Society. Big Ray — six feet, a muscular 185 pounds — used to run the quaint Red Star North Bookstore in Portland and was active in SCAR, the prison-reform group. Their "gang" includes wives and children and friends. They were traced to farmhouses in Pennsylvania and Vermont, but the FBI always arrived too late. As these

photos suggest, Levasseur and Manning have reputations as good fathers, making sure under very difficult circumstances that their kids get a good education and proper medical care.

Thomas Manning

Teaching Deaf Kids the Ways of the World

Robert Kelley was a man who, basically, ran the state government's Baxter School for the Deaf in Falmouth for about fifteen years — until a newspaper expose in 1982 determined that he had spent many of

Robert Kelley

those years sexually abusing a number of the boys, in addition to physically mistreating some of them. The state attorney general determined that this activity had, in fact, gone on, but decided not to press charges because of the stress former Baxter students would have to undergo on the stand. The statute of limitations was also a problem. Kelly, however, was fired, as were a few other administrators.

Governor Joseph Brennan

Giving Away the State Treasury to the Military-Industrial Complex

Joe Brennan made United States history in 1981 when he herded a sheeplike legislature into special session, presented them with inaccurate information, and obtained almost-unanimous passage of a bill giving — not loaning — but *giving away* about $20 million in public funds to a private conglomerate, the Congoleum Corporation, owner of the Bath Iron Works, the state's largest employer and a Brennan campaign contributor. This was a bribe, eagerly solicited by BIW, to get them to build a drydock in Portland instead of Boston. Opposition surfaced in the form of puny Common Cause, the *soi-disant* "citizens' lobby," who, however, were massively outspent by BIW in a referendum campaign over the bonds to finance the deal. Voters approved the give-away by fifty-eight percent. Common Cause then took the state to court, but lost when the Supreme Judicial Court of Maine said, hey, it's okay to give away the taxpayers' money to big business — it's done all the time.

"Even Maine Failed as Sanctuary for Scientist Hounded Across World"

Guy Gannett Newspapers

headline of 1967
article on Wilhelm Reich
in *Maine Sunday Telegram*

Wilhem Reich (top photo), famous psychoanalyst disciple of Freud, free-sex advocate, inventor of the orgone box, author of *The Function of the Orgasm* and *The Mass Psychology of Facism*, inventor of the cloudbuster (bottom photo) to make rain, came to a bad end in Maine in the intolerant fifties. Tired of being spied on by the Food & Drug Administration, which thought he was corrupting America's youth, he built a stone fortress on a hilltop in Rangeley which today serves as his museum. Open in the summer, the museum has prim young women who take you around his laboratory talking of orgasms.

In 1953 Reich made rain for Downeast blueberry farmers. He got paid for his services. In 1954, seeing UFOs, he shot them down with the cloudbuster. He thought that Air Force jets flying overhead soon thereafter was President Eisenhower's way of saying thanks. In 1956 the FDA arrested him. The agents destroyed his orgone accumulators and burned his books. He was tried in Portland and sentenced to federal prison, where, in the Lewisburg Federal Penitentiary, Pennsylvania, he literally died of a broken heart in 1957.

Mark Melnicove

6 Sex

One might be of the opinion, because of the cold, that there is little sex in Maine. Sex for obvious reasons is associated with heat. But those herds of yellow monsters, school-buses, indicate that something has been going on to propagate the race of the granite-headed. Someone has been frigging, as we say to be elegant. Perhaps, even, *making love*, even though the weather is so fickle that you can't take off the woolies for much more than the fourth of July weekend — which explains to some extent why a lot of children in Maine are born approximately nine months from that date, or so the rumors would have it.

Of course, in this day and age, people have

heated, sometimes overheated, houses and frigging can go on even in a blizzard — in fact it sometimes does just to spite the elements. Some connoisseurs suggest that there is nothing like it when it is forty below, the wind blowing fifty miles a hour, and the snow coming down in fistfulls.

From the gay beaches of Ogunquit to the nude beaches of Skowhegan, not all coupling is meant to produce children and every now and then it is a pleasure. Be fruitful and multiply, says the commandment, but even in a Puritan land occasionally some joy is snuck in. Leo Connellan, famous Maine poet, has written movingly of the effect of Maine gravel on his knees during a particularly pleasant episode in Rockland.

One of the most interesting locations for sex in Maine is the sauna. Here is a semipublic place where sex takes place with the joyfully illicit feeling that the same thing is happening on either side of you. You may be wrong. Some say that 200-degree heat is not that ideal for romance, but, on the other hand, sweat has its advantages. If the sauna you are attending has a pool, you often see more than you paid for. Saunas are prevalent in Maine because of the Finnish stonecutters who came to Knox and Oxford Counties. Many of the high school classmates of one of the authors first saw the naked bodies of the opposite sex in the saunas of their Finnish classmates. The commercial saunas started up with one or two in the South Paris area and have now spread to many parts of the state.

Cultured gays from out of state flock every summer to Ogunquit for fun in the sun. There are a number of clubs and hotels that cater to this trade and make a good living at it. This is prob-

TYPICAL *MAINE TIMES* PERSONALS

SENSITIVE Christian man wishes to find very sensitive, slender Christian woman who is musical. Get to play my organ and one-third of collection-plate receipts. Just a straight business arrangement. I pray for acceptance.

FAT BROAD, divorced, 6 children, 42, smoker, boozer, would like someone to support me. I am tired of working in the shoe factory. Almost anyone with money will do.

DIVORCED WHITE MALE, 40, no children, would like to meet someone with children under 5. Object: a good meal. Kids getting in the way of your lifestyle? I am an expert in roasting children; they make the tastiest meal imaginable. If this goes right, maybe a relationship can develop. Please send picture of the kids and your phone number.

Bangor Daily News

In 1975 women's libbers in Bangor required Paul Bunyan to have a vasectomy

ably the only town in Maine where one is likely to see male handholding on the street. One used to see it at the Blue Boy Bookstore in Portland (now closed), where there were convenient holes between the booths.

Maine was where the young Neal Dow, soon to be the king of the Prohibition movement, in 1834 formed the Young Men's Morality Society and got a bill passed against "houses of ill fame." There used to be whorehouses of good dimension, what with the sailors and loggers and other rootless men. There was the Sky Blue House in Bangor and all the little candy shops on Sea Street in Rockland. The pinnacle of enthusiasm about these places happened early — in 1825 — when the infamous Portland Whorehouse Riot occurred. One person was killed and the whole town was in an uproar.

In some cities there are quite a few greasy sex-aide shoppes, where one can buy the odd dildo or movie. One of the more celebrated was the Fantasy Bookshoppe in Brunswick located strategically close to the Brunswick Naval Air Station and Bowdoin College. There, for a dollar, one could see a ten-minute movie. This has now been replaced, to the chagrin of some, by a laundromat. What symbolism!

There have always been penitential aides. The Maine Maritime Museum in Bath has in its collection a piece of scrimshaw (etched sperm whale's tooth) with a pornographic message and drawing on it. It is of the homosexual kind. This confirms certain suspicions by leftist maritime historians that four years on a whaling ship left plenty of time for fiddlin' in the fo'castle. Bath is known as the town that launched ten thousand ships. The sailors we so proudly trace our roots to were perhaps bi-dextro. There are some strange bawdy lyrics in sea chanteys that also give this indication.

Maine locales: On a sailboat...on a granite ledge on top of Cadillac Mountain...on a squeaky bed in a summer camp...on a cool moss bed beside the Appalachian Trail...in a snowbank after a particularly hot sauna.

...And let us not forget the old Maine tradition of a peculiar use of ice at the moment of orgasm.

The Great Portland WHOREHOUSE RIOT

Maine seaports were noted for their accomodations of the sexual needs of the thousands of sailors that passed through in the nineteenth century. In 1825 in the city of Portland there were a number of houses of ill-fame along the waterfront. But not everybody in Portland was liberal about such places. Early in that year several times "laboring men, truckmen and boys" had torn down some of the nests and burned others.

Then on a Saturday night in November, 1825, according to the contemporary *Weekly Argus* "the *reformers* attacked a two story house on Fore Street, occupied by a colored barber by the name of Gray. Gray had been convicted at the Common Pleas Court of keeping a house of ill-fame, and had appealed to the Supreme Court which is now in session, and in which he has also been convicted the present week. But the mob chose to render more speedy justice than the laws would do, and accordingly on Saturday night they threw a few rocks into Gray's house, broke the windows, &c, but either from want of sufficient forces or from meeting more resistance than they expected, they desisted 'till Monday evening, when they renewed their attacks with increased forces. In the mean time Gray had armed himself with guns and other weapons. He and his family, with some others remained in the house. In the course of the assault, the mob fired guns into the house, and guns were fired from the house upon the mob. Which fired first, we are not informed. One man in the street, an Englishman, by the name of Joseph Fuller, was killed almost instantly and six or eight others were wounded, some severely. After this the crowd soon dispersed."

Gray was tried for manslaughter and acquitted in May of 1826. It was shown that Fuller had been a leader of the mob and had sworn to kill Gray.

More Sex in Maine

Portland's Exchange Street, now an outpost of the fernbar and brick-wall beau-tique set, used to be a lot more authentic: It used to be the whorehouse district, the centerpiece being the sailors' Silver House with its famous Madam Silver Tits (don't ask us why).

Even in the authors' memories, the Exchange Street region was littered with low-life taverns that would wilt a fern in seconds. Notable was The Crow's Nest, where for years the favorite stripper, and by far the best, was Stanley. That's right, Stanley. When Stanley took off his/her clothes, those at the bar who had had enough beer didn't seem to care about Stanley's anatomical persuasion, whatever it might be.

Let us speak the unspeakable. It is a well-known fact that, in the equipment line, Maine men are *built* differently.

Women, next time you visit some quaint seaside village, check out the men unloading those trawlers. To be blunt, take a good hard look at what's below the gunwales. What will you see? Well, you'll see the biggest *cleavage* since your last Elizabeth Taylor movie. Maine men are so proud of their rear ends that they like to show them off. In Maine, it is the *men* who have the *derrieres* to make Rudolph Nureyev jump for jealousy.

You'd hardly think the water was cold. This is Seawall Beach

NUDE BEACHES

DRAKE'S BEACH, Wells

MOODY'S BEACH, Moody

SEAWALL BEACH, Popham

ROCKS NEAR HAYSTACK CRAFTS SCHOOL, Deer Isle

BEACH NEAR LAKEWOOD THEATRE, Skowhegan

First came the fashion of wearing running shorts *outside* of long underpants. The latest clothes craze among the outdoorsy set in Maine is to wear down-filled bras and jockstraps *over* turtlenecks or boxer shorts. It does serve a practical purpose in keeping the respective family jewels comfortably warm. (Available from Maine Sport in Camden and Rockland.)

PORTLAND PROSTITUTES TAKE BLOWS

A Portland prostitute propositions Parkhurst Volvo

In recent years Portland's prostitutes were subjected to two blows from which they have only partially recovered. The first was the demolishing of Dunkin' Donuts on Congress Square, which was *the* pickup point for this kind of amatory action. The second was the state legislature's passage of a "johns law," which allows police to pick up men who make the mistake of soliciting policewomen disguised as hookers.

The consequences of getting arrested as a john are $250 in a fine and your name in the papers. The clergy supported the johns law's passage, and many observers thought it fitting that the first person arrested for soliciting a prostitute was a minister.

The demise of Dunkin' Donuts has meant that hooking is now more ambulatory: the section of Congress (how aptly named) from Congress Square to Longfellow Square (also aptly named, when you think about it), is where the traffic is heaviest. The Parisienne Sauna is located just off Longfellow Square. A masseuse there was once found guilty of soliciting bonus business by "hand gesture," a precedent in Maine law.

Solicitations have turned to other novel means. One woman who ran an "erotigrams" strip service was arrested in Portland after also advertising in the Portland papers for her "escort service" which allegedly provided certain fringe benefits.

Reliable sources say there are one to two hundred prostitutes in Portland during the summer season, with as many as fifty pimps. In the winter, the prostitutes may be diminished to fewer than fifty. The older ones generally come "from away," from outside the state. The younger — down to twelve years old and younger — are runaways from their homes in Maine and elsewhere.

Girlie-show veterans at the Skowhegan Fair. The bumper sticker partly in view has the famous Maine lumbermen's silvicultural expression: "Save a tree, eat a beaver"

Maine's Cheapest Thrills

Girlie shows at Maine country fairs have been a time-honored tradition whose time may have passed, at least for a while, because of a newspaper expose in 1981.

The girlie-show secret was amazingly well kept considering that thousands of Maine men have been involved in keeping it. Wives have been annoyed or amused for years at their husbands going inside the carnival tent to take a gander at what they assumed were young ladies revealing themselves. Little did they know that things were a mite stronger than that.

Reporters Jeff Beebe and Scot Lehigh visited the Topsham Fair's Hollywood Palace and reported the action on the front page of the Brunswick *Times Record:* It ranged from an unusual use of corncobs and — can you believe it? — beer cans to four men having sex with one woman at once, a feat that verges on the

athletic, to say the least. Several protesting men were pinned down by their buddies while the women raped them — it's the only word that can be used — orally. At one point four women leaped off the stage and let themselves be copulated with indiscriminately by the crowd of shouting, frantic men. "For $4 each, spectators became participants," read the headline above the newspaper story. Cheap thrills, indeed.

Well, that story created a bit of a stir, and the Hollywood Palace was closed down. Since then, too, the Real Maine Girlie Show has been harder to find than lice at a Ladies Aid Society tea.

While many people are happy about that fact, many are not. Reporter Beebe tells of a man who called him the day after his article appeared and the show was shut down. "You spoiled the only fun we had all year," he complained.

Mark Melnicove

Girlie shows may be on the way out, but the legendary Holly, in Lewiston, lives on — Maine's most famous strip-tease joint

MOSCOW AIR FORCE STATION

CONUS OTH-B (ERS) TRANSMIT SITE

U.S. AIR FORCE PROJECT

WARNING
U.S. GOVERNMENT PROPERTY
NO TRESPASSING

CONSTRUCTION UNDER SUPERVISION OF

ELECTRONIC SYSTEMS DIVISION

SYSTEM CONTRACTOR - GENERAL ELECTRIC CO.

MAINE AREA CONTRACTORS

PRENTISS & CARLISLE CO., INC.	BANGOR, ME.	CENTRAL CITY SHEET METAL, INC.	BANGOR, ME.
BLUE ROCK INDUSTRIES	WESTBROOK, ME.	NATIONAL REFRIGERATION CO. INC.	PLYMOUTH, ME.
JORDAN GORRILL ASSOCIATES	BANGOR, ME.	GAMEWELL	NORTH HAMPTON, N.H.
P.L. JONES & SONS	ELLSWORTH, ME.	BERNARD CATES	BINGHAM, ME.
CENTRAL MAINE POWER CO	AUGUSTA, ME.	HANSEN MACHINE SHOP	BINGHAM, ME.
THE SHERIDAN CORP	FAIRFIELD, ME.	BILL MELCHER	BINGHAM, ME.
VALLEY PLUMBING & HEATING	BINGHAM, ME.	DANA W. BARTLETT	CHERRYFIELD, ME.
NEW ENGLAND TELEPHONE	WATERVILLE, ME.	AL ZIMBA	FAIRFIELD, ME.
S.L.F. INC.	SKOWHEGAN, ME.	F.H. CHASE, INC.	ALTON, MASS.
CIANBRO CORP	PITTSFIELD, ME.	FRANK BROCHU	BINGHAM, ME.
SEAWARD CONST. CO., INC.	KITTERY, ME.	WM. C. LANCASTER	SOLON, ME.
THOR ELECTRIC	NEWINGTON, N.H.	SECURITY FENCE CO.	PITTSFIELD, ME.
JOHNSON CONTROLS INC.	PORTLAND, ME	ABINGTON CONSTRUCTORS	N. HAMPTON, N.H.

Even small machine shops in Bingham, Maine, are part of the military-industrial complex

7 *Military*

To the Kremlin, Maine is no Vacationland. No handsome coast of fishing harbors, no vastness of forest and lakes and mountains. To them Maine is a threat; and a target of major significance.
                                                    —*Maine Sunday Telegram*
                                                    Aug. 2, 1981

Stephen B. Nichols

Have you ever wondered what happens to Maine's beaches after the tourists leave?

The following list of the Top 25 nuclear targets in Maine has been smuggled out of the Soviet Union by an *Uncensored Guide* reporter who, for obvious reasons, wishes to remain nameless — but it is *not* Samantha Smith. This is the first time any list as accurate as this has been published, and although we are proud to provide the public service we are also horrified by what it reveals.

For years we have heard that the Kremlin had Loring Air Force Base, Kittery, Bath-Brunswick, Portland, Cutler, Lewiston, Augusta and Bangor in its sights, but we, along with most other Mainers, thought that was it. As can be seen from the list, however, the Kremlin has much more in mind.

Mainers beware: Those of you interested in survival will want to study the map we have provided

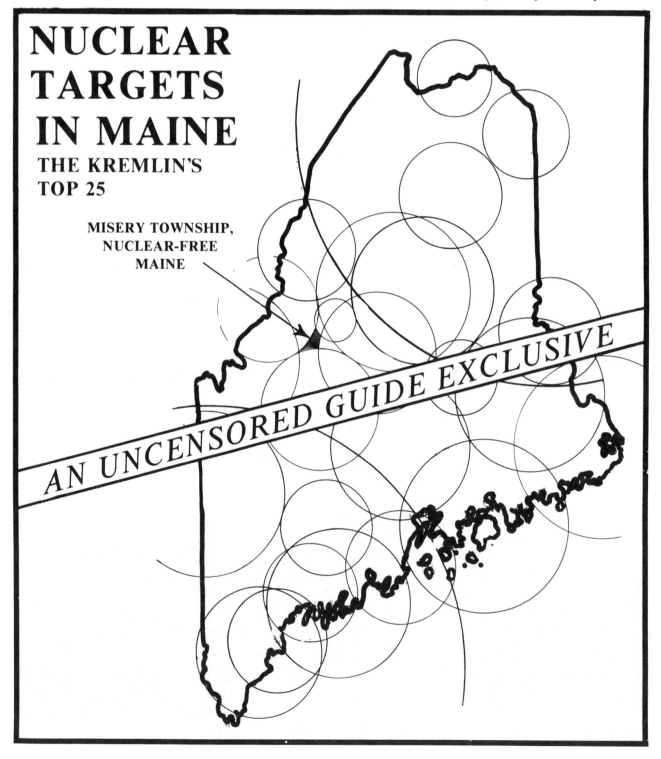

NUCLEAR TARGETS IN MAINE
THE KREMLIN'S TOP 25

MISERY TOWNSHIP, NUCLEAR-FREE MAINE

AN UNCENSORED GUIDE EXCLUSIVE

Guy Gannett Newspapers

B-52s at Loring Air Force Base

very closely. Nuclear-Free Maine is indicated (the center of which is Misery Township). You may consider moving to Misery before it is too late.

1. *LORING AIR FORCE BASE, Limestone:* Number one target because it is the only U.S. base in Maine that is equipped to drop nuclear bombs on Russian soil. Loring's B-52 bombers will only be able to deliver these bombs, however, if they get off the ground in time. This will not occur if the Russians destroy the B-52s first. It would only take ten-fifteen minutes or less for nuclear bombs launched from Russian submarines in the Atlantic Ocean to reach Loring. Loring's top brass know this and, even in their "best-case scenarios," they figure only a few of their B-52s will make it off the ground to begin the dangerous eight-hour flight to Russia.

Also in the neighborhood say goodbye to:

Aroostook County; parts of *Piscataquis, Somerset, Penobscot* and *Washington* counties; parts of the Canadian provinces of *New Brunswick* and *Quebec*; the *St. John River*, etc. (The Soviets are not going to go light on the bombs on Loring.)

2. *BRUNSWICK NAVAL AIR STATION (BNAS), Brunswick:* East-Coast headquarters of the U.S. antisubmarine warfare program. BNAS has nuclear bombs, too, but they are puny in comparison to Loring's and are meant to be deployed against Russian submarines and not Russian cities. Destruction of BNAS is a critical step for the Kremlin if their submarines hope to pass unmolested through Atlantic Ocean waters and successfully launch their missiles toward Maine.

Also in the neighborhood say goodbye to:

Peary-Macmillan Arctic Museum, Bowdoin College: Unique collection of artifacts of the two famous polar explorers. These artifacts would be useful during the "nuclear winter," if only they could survive the heat of the Soviet bombs.

3. *KITTERY-PORTSMOUTH NAVAL SHIPYARD, Kittery:* The only East-Coast Navy shipyard charged with the responsibility of repairing and overhauling America's nuclear submarine fleet. A Soviet attack on Kittery would not only destroy the shipyard, but also the submarines that happened to be there for modernization or repair. These submarines are powered by nuclear reactors and their radioactive elements would be dispersed far and wide into the surrounding southern Maine and New Hampshire countryside by the Soviet blasts.

Suicide Is Painless?

It seems fitting that Loring Air Force Base, Maine's Number One nuclear target, is named after someone who committed suicide.

Charles J. Loring, Jr., of Portland, was a Korean War fighter pilot who deliberately crashed his wounded F-80 jet into enemy antiaircraft fire, kamikaze-style, on November 22, 1952. This desperate act so captured the imagination of his fellow Mainers that the I-295 highway, which runs past Portland, and is used by many suicidal drivers, was also named after him.

Is there any other way to describe Loring Air Force Base's planned B-52 attacks on the Soviet Union than suicidal?

Also in the neighborhood say goodbye to:
Piscataqua River Bridge: Important escape route from or into Maine via I-95.

4. *BATH IRON WORKS, Bath:* Makes largest "Made in Maine" product — Navy guided-missile frigates and destroyers. Twenty-seventh largest defense contractor in all of U.S.A. Its Kennebec River port could be used as an emergency Navy base, but won't be if the Kremlin gets to it first.

Also in the neighborhood say goodbye to:
Toy Soldier, 116 Front St., Bath: Military games, books and models on sale here would be useful when trying to reconstruct U.S. military forces from scratch after a nuclear war.

5. *FAMILY ESTATE OF VICE-PRESIDENT GEORGE BUSH, Kennebunkport:* Command and control headquarters for man who is only a heartbeat away from the presidency. Bush could give the orders for a nuclear war against the Russians from this outpost if the President is dead.

6. *CASPER WEINBERGER'S HOUSE, Somesville:* Summertime command and control headquarters for the U.S. Secretary of Defense. Weinburger could give the orders for a nuclear war from this outpost if the President, Vice-President, Speaker of the House, etc. are dead.

Also in the neighborhood say goodbye to:
Acadia National Park, Mt. Desert Island: Popular American playground, once controlled by the rich, now controlled by back-to-the-earth types, a few remaining natives, and automobile-dependent sightseers.

7. *CUTLER NET, Cutler:* The most important military communications system in Maine. It will tell U.S. nuclear submarines when to go to war and destroy the Soviet Union. It can communicate with the submarines because of its two-million-watt VLF transmitter, the "most powerful radio station in the world." Its twenty-six towers, ranging from 250 to 950 feet, give the Russians plenty to aim at.

Also in the neighborhood say goodbye to:
Machias Seal Island: Ancestral home of the puffin.

8. *MOUNT KATAHDIN, Baxter State Park:* Large, easy-to-strike target. Symbol of all that is good about Maine. The "Evil Empire," because they hate the good, have their sights set on Katahdin.

Also in the neighborhood say goodbye to:
A lot of moose.

9. *AMERICAN LEGION HEADQUARTERS, Waterville:* Command and control headquarters for Maine's powerful military lobby and propaganda machine. Feared by the Soviets almost as much as the Pentagon itself.

Also in the neighborhood say goodbye to:
Scott Paper, Winslow: Toilet paper manufacturer. Extremely important facility to "wipe out."

Typical well-guarded security area at Brunswick Naval Air Station. Behind the fence on the left are nuclear bombs

10. *STETSON, a town in Penobscot County:* Although voting at its March, 1983, town meeting to become America's fifth "Nuclear Free Zone," Stetson (pop. 620) voted again two months later in May and decided it didn't want to be nuclear-free anymore. The Kremlin, never skipping a beat, has apparently decided to give Stetson what it wants.

11. *SUGARLOAF, U.S.A., Carrabassett Valley:* Training ground for future U.S. Olympic ski champions. Russians want to make sure they are killed so that U.S. won't win any more Olympics.

12. *BATH IRON WORKS, Portland:* One of a handful of Navy yards capable of repairing and modernizing destroyers, cruisers and aircraft carriers, and converting large commercial ships into military rapid-deployment vessels. Its 844-long dry dock makes it easy to "see" for the stupidest "smart" missile.

Also in the neighborhood say goodbye to:

Defense Contract Administration, 151 Forest Ave.: Administers over one billion dollars worth of defense contracts to Maine businesses every year. Kremlin would rather see them starve.

13. *MAINE YANKEE, Wiscasset*: Maine's largest nuclear reactor. All of the spent fuel the plant has burned since it opened in 1972 is still stored on site. Maine Yankee's radioactive poisons will persist thousands of times longer in the environment than those of the nuclear bomb that hits it (not that it makes a whole hell of a lot of difference).

Also in the neighborhood say goodbye to:

Fort Edgecomb: Built in 1808 to defend Maine Yankees from attack.

14. *OVER-THE-HORIZON RADAR Operations Center, Bangor.*

15. *OVER-THE-HORIZON RADAR Transmitter, Moscow.*

16. *OVER-THE-HORIZON RADAR Receiver, Township 19.* Scheduled to be operational by 1987, the Over-the-Horizon Radar is supposed to give early warning of incoming Soviet bombers. Destruction of the O-T-H Radar before Soviet bombers enter U.S. airspace is therefore an important Soviet priority.

Also in the neighborhood say goodbye to:

"Remember the Maine" Memorial, Bangor: Monument includes the original shield from the battleship Maine, blown up in Cuba in 1898. Local people claim the shield will provide pro-

Get the message?

Nuclear Depth Charges on the Maine Coast

The Navy doesn't admit there are nuclear bombs at the Naval Air Station in Brunswick. Ask them about the nuclear depth charges stored there and they say: "It is the Department of Defense position to neither confirm or deny the presence of nuclear weapons at any of its facilities."

The Russians have some spectacular photographs of these bombs, taken by their spy satellites, but, unfortunately, in spite of numerous requests, the *Uncensored Guide* was unable to obtain them.

Most of the time these bombs gather dust at the station, unknown to the passing tourists driving on Route 24 to Orrs and Bailey Islands. The Marines assigned to guard them have little to do but count the particles of dust as they settle on the warheads and stare longingly at nearby New Meadows Cemetery.

The Navy does dust the bombs off every so often, load them onto the Orion P-3C airplanes, and fly them over the Maine countryside on their way out to pester Russian submarines in the Atlantic. The bombs can pack a punch. Even if they missed a Russian sub by five miles, they'd still destroy it. The same goes for any fishermen who got in the way.

The Orions prove the old adage that you can't judge an airplane by its fuselage. Their dull grey exteriors and lethargic-sounding propellers give them a vintage, fifties appearance. Yet, the Navy says they are the most sophisticated anti-submarine warfare (ASW) plane in the world today.

Never heard of ASW? The military doesn't like to mention it, but not because it's embarassed to be flying nuclear bombs over innocent Maine citizens or because it is Top Secret. It's just that ASW is one area of the arms race where we are ahead of the Russians.

tection from a nuclear attack, but Fidel Castro isn't so sure.

The Great Heath, Columbia: Largest raised bog in Maine, home of rare flowers. Great Heath peat could supply energy needs of the Over-the-Horizon receiver if all other sources fail.

Scott Paper Company clear-cuts: Scott is the largest landowner near the Moscow O-T-H Transmitter. Clear-cuts are beautiful in comparison to what the area will look like once the Russians get finished with it.

17. *OLD SPECK MOUNTAIN, Grafton Notch State Park:*

18. *SPECKLED MOUNTAIN, White Mountain National Forest:* Kremlin has targeted these two mountains because of their proximity to Green Beret "unconventional warfare" training grounds. This western area of Maine is prized by the Pentagon because of the similarity of its terrain to the European "theater."

Also in the neighborhood say goodbye to:

Kezar Lake, Lovell: Called "one of the world's three most beautiful lakes" by *National Geographic.* Soviet military want to destroy this lake to prove they are as hard-nosed as the Americans.

Hikers on the Appalachian Trail: Shelters on the trail provide little protection from nuclear blast.

19. *ANDOVER EARTH STATION, Andover:* Telstar satellite communications terminus built by AT&T in 1965. Serves as an important communications link between the U.S. and its NATO allies. Despised by the Kremlin for the role it played in the 1969 moon landing.

Also in the neighborhood say goodbye to:

Lovejoy Bridge: Escape route from Andover on Maine's shortest covered bridge.

20. *PRATT & WHITNEY, North Berwick:* Maine's largest aircraft factory. P&W is manufacturer of world's most sophisticated jet engines for customers such as Boeing, McDonnell Douglas, General Dynamics and (the Russians are quick to note) the Pentagon.

Also in the neighborhood say goodbye to:

Sarah Orne Jewett House, South Berwick: Of this house, the world-renowned novelist wrote: "I was born here and I hope to die here, leaving the lilac bushes still green and growing, and all the chairs in their places." Russians have no sympathy for reactionary bourgeois Maine literary landmarks.

CRISIS RELOCATION

Assuming there is any warning given before the start of a nuclear war (becoming less likely in our computerized world), then the Federal Emergency Management Agency (FEMA) would attempt to move approximately 150 million Americans from "probable target sites" to "crisis relocation centers" at less probable target sites.

For example, this game of nuclear musical chairs would see Massachusetts residents from Roxbury, Jamaica Plains and Back Bay move to Augusta, even though Augusta would probably be bombed, too. East Boston would move en masse to Gardiner. West Roxbury would move to Winthrop, North Fenway would move to Farmingdale. Beacon Hill would move to Litchfield (*Don't forget to pack your lunch!*)

"I want the people of Boston to understand they are coming to a small town with very limited facilities," warns Dr. Mary Skorapa, Litchfield's health officer. "I think it would be ridiculous."

According to the FEMA plans, each Maine town would be given a code letter. In case of a nuclear war, road signs would be hastily posted along the highways leading to Maine. These signs would display the code letters of the Maine towns. The 800,000 Massachusetts residents fleeing to Maine would have to remember the number to get to their assigned town. Mistakes could be fatal. Imagine the dismay of South Fenway residents who accidentally exited at Brunswick instead of Randolph. Brunswick is guaranteed to be bye-bye in the first wave of missiles.

Massachusetts residents don't need to worry about getting lost in Maine. As Dr. Skorapa points out, "If there were any real trouble, most of them wouldn't get here anyway."

Ninety thousand Mainers would also be moved around from high priority targets to lower priority ones. Brewer, Orrington and Holden would go to Ellsworth. Hermon would go to Corinna. North Bangor, Kenduskeag and Glenburn would go to Dover-Foxcroft. The rest of Bangor would go to Dexter, Millinocket, Howland and Lincoln (those without cars can walk).

21. *MAREMONT CORPORATION, Saco:* Number One manufacturer of machine guns for the Pentagon. Maine's second largest defense contractor (Bath Iron Works is Number One).

Also in the neighborhood say goodbye to:

Old Orchard Beach: Quebecois crisis relocation center.

22. *PORTLAND VALVE INC., Scarborough:* Number One manufacturer of ball valves for Navy nuclear submarines. These valves are not sized to fit Russian submarines, therefore Kremlin considers them expendable.

Also in the neighborhood say goodbye to:

Prout's Neck: Crisis-relocation center for upper-class, white Republican businessmen who run America.

23. *FAIRCHILD DIGITAL, South Portland:* Makes silicon chips for Pentagon missile guidance systems in its new, 179,000-square-foot Aerospace and Defense Building.

Also in the neighborhood say goodbye to:

Portland Head Light, Fort Williams: Its 100-foot-high hurricane deck is a great place to catch an early glimpse of the incoming nuclear missiles.

24. *DIELECTRIC COMMUNICATIONS, Raymond.* Founded in 1960, Dielectric is the "grandaddy" of the approximately one dozen microwave defense contractors in the Sebago Lake area.

Also in the neighborhood say goodbye to:

Sebago Lake: Portland's water supply and a great place to catch salmon.

25. *COMMANDER PATROL WING FIVE, U.S. ATLANTIC FLEET, Topsham:* Command center for Brunswick Naval Air Station, across the Androscoggin River in Topsham.

Also in the neighborhood say goodbye to:

Mt. Ararat: Although named after the mountain on which Noah placed his ark, area residents have never seriously considered using their mountain as a crisis relocation center, and it's just as well.

Secret Russian air base found in Maine

Fried Potatoes

The Soviet attack on Loring in spudland would be the most complex waged against any Maine target. One writer has described the attack this way:

"(There would be) a relatively low-altitude, high-yield airburst over the base to cause damage, perhaps a groundburst to vaporize runways and facilities, and a series of airbursts in a fan-shaped pattern running 50 to 100 miles from the base, from northwest to northeast. The airbursts closest to the base, from five to 10 miles, will be detonated anywhere from 6,000 to 10,000 feet, to catch bombers climbing to their operating altitudes. Those airbursts farther away will be set higher. Anyone living within this fan-shaped area is in imminent danger from the direct effects of the weaponry, from the moment of the attack. A major intercontinental bomber base today can count on being targeted for three to 12 warheads or more, which makes a vast area north of Loring very dangerous. If the attacker is profligate in the use of his weapons, then the airbursts may be extended in a full circle of 50 to 100 miles in radius, in all directions from the base. Should any of the base remain operational despite the onslaught, the immediate vicinity can count upon being targeted for a subsequent groundburst to finish the job, and this may happen days, weeks, or months after the outbreak of war."

from *Second Sunrise: Nuclear War: The Untold Story*, by Michael Pogodzinski, Thorndike Press, 1983

3 Famous Maine Poets Describe "THE DAY AFTER" in Maine

There's nothing like a night sitting around the fire reading the great Maine poets — Millay, Longfellow, Robinson...

Their words harken back to another age, a more peaceful time before atomic bombs were invented.

But what if...? What if these great Maine poets were alive today? What if they survived a nuclear war between the superpowers (as impossible as that might seem)? What kinds of poems would they write then?

To answer this question, the *Uncensored Guide* called their spirits back from the dead.

MY LOST YOUTH

Often I stumble through Portland town
   That is ashes by the sea;
Often on my hands and knees go down
The ruins of that dear old town,
   And my youth flies away from me.
      And a verse of a Soviet song
      Is haunting my memory still:
      "A bomb's will is the Kremlin's will,
And the drought of war is a long, dry drought."

Henry Wadsworth Longfellow

NO CHANCE FOR RENASCENCE

The world blows up on every side
Blacker than the heart that's fried;
Above the world is poisoned sky —
Radioactive clouds are flying high.
The bomb can push the sea and land
Farther away on either hand;
The bomb can split the sky in two,
And let the face of grief fall through.
East and West will pinch the heart
As uranium atoms split apart,
And he whose soul is damned — the sky
Will cave in on him by and by.

Edna St. Vincent Millay

EROS TYRANNOUS

The falling bomb inaugurates
   The reign of mass confusion;
The pressing weight reiterates
   This blast is no illusion;
And home, where passion lived and died,
There is no place for us to hide,
While all the town and countryside
   Black out in grim conclusion.

Edward Arlington Robinson

Mark Melnicove

Somewhere-Over-the-Horizon radar transmitting in Moscow

SOMEWHERE OVER THE HORIZON

Around 1970 the Air Force figured they'd give the Kremlin something else to shoot at, so they began making plans to build the Over-the-Horizon Radar in Maine.

This technological marvel got its name because it "sees" over the horizon and not in a straight line like conventional radar. It does this by beaming a high-frequency microwave signal up to the ionosphere (anywhere from fifty to 250 miles above the earth). The signal is deflected off the ionosphere and comes back down to earth as much as 1,800 miles from Maine. If the signal meets up with an airplane, it will be deflected by the plane back up to the ionosphere and then return to Maine where cool and collected Air Force operators will receive and interpret it. If the plane is a Soviet bomber on its way to the U.S., the Air Force could have as much as two hours to keep track of the bomber before it dropped its bombs on American soil. In today's nuclear, trigger-happy, missile-happy world, two hours is a long time.

Two hours is so long that by the time the Soviet bombers reached American shores there might not be anything left to drop their bombs on. Faster-arriving Soviet intercontinental ballistic missiles and submarine-launched missiles might have already disfigured the American landscape so much that the last-to-arrive bombers might think they have discovered the moon and not their intended target.

These technicalities aside, the Over-the-Horizon Radar is a brilliant invention. It has three main components:

1) *The transmitter*, that part of the radar which starts things off by sending the aforementioned signal up to the ionosphere. The transmitter is located on the outer fringes of Moscow (not the capital of Russia, heh, heh, but a sparsely settled town near Bingham, best known for its many acres of Scott Paper Company clear-cuts). The decision to locate in a town called Moscow was probably not easy for the Air Force to make. The citizens of Moscow were excited to hear that the giant microwave oven was moving into town. They reasoned it would be a new, inexpensive way to cook their bean-hole suppers. What the Air Force didn't tell them, though, was that intense microwave radiation can cause cataracts and has been known to break down the body's immune system. *Uncensored Guide* statisticians are therefore watching the Moscow population closely to see if cases of AIDS break out.

2) *The receiver* receives the returning signal and is capable of distinguishing it from birdsong at least fifty percent of the time. The receiver is located in Washington County's T19, one of the 200-plus townships in Maine that are so "unorganized" that they haven't even got it together yet to come up with a regular name for themselves. T19 is bordered by Northfield, Centerville, Columbia Falls, Columbia and Ts 18, 24 and 25. This is the center of the blueberry barrens, the economic backbone of Washington County. When plans for the receiver were announced, the Air Force said they would have to clear-cut 300-plus acres of prime blueberry bushes to make way for it. When outraged T19 blueberry growers suggested the Air Force locate the receiver in T18 instead (the Air Force used it as a bombing range during World War II), they were told T18 sloped in the wrong direction and the cost of reorienting the land in the right direction was prohibitively expensive — not usually a consideration for the Pentagon.

3) *The operations center* interprets the signal and is being built in Bangor at the airport. The center will employ 450 people. The high paying, high-tech jobs will no doubt go to out-of-staters and the minimum-wage security guard and janitorial jobs will no doubt go to Bangor natives. Of course, there may be *no jobs*, since, by the time the radar is finished in 1987, it may be obsolete.

Ah, the Healthy State of ME

The myth of Maine includes the myth that it is a healthy place to live. However:

• Maine has the highest rate of death from heart disease in the nation.

• Maine probably has the worst dental health in the country. "New England has by far the worst dental health" in the United States, and "usually when economic factors are low, correspondingly dental health is low," says a state dental health official. Maine is the poorest state in New England (and in the country). Thus it is reasonable to conclude that Mainers have the worst chompers in the U.S. (In some areas a new set of teeth is a prized high-school graduation gift.)

• If you live in a mill town you are twenty-four percent more likely to be hospitalized for asthma than if you don't. "All the paper towns have very poor health," says a state health official.

• Maine has fewer doctors and dentists per 100,000 civilian population than any other New England state.

• The average lifetime for men (67.24 years) and women (74.85 years) in Maine is lowest among all New England states.

• The state's chief health officer, Dr. William Nersesian, says his "biggest worry" is petroleum products in the groundwater (11 million gallons leaking from underground storage tanks each year). "Almost every part of the state has some kind of contaminant," he also points out.

• Although the federal government found "no association...between leukemia incidence and residence near the [Wiscasset Maine Yankee nuclear] power plant," Dr. Irwin Bross, Director of Biostatistics of the Roswell Park Memorial Institute, Buffalo, N.Y., found a "drastic increase" in leukemia in southern Maine during the 1970s. "The increased risk of leukemia may possibly (though not certainly) be related to the Maine Yankee reactor." Another study found the coastal leukemia rate "has more than doubled."

• Maine has the seventh highest cancer rate in the U.S.

• A 1983 report by the state's Department of Human Services said that cigarette smoking in Maine "accounts for more than 1,800 deaths and at least $10 million worth of excess medical care each year." Mainers smoke an estimated 114 million packs of cigarettes each year.

• State researchers have found that Eastport, Calais and Jonesport are the towns with the worst health; Berwick, Fort Fairfield and York have the best.

• Maine's infant mortality rate during the first year of life may be the lowest in the country, but this may be because blacks have twice the infant mortality of whites and there are few blacks in Maine.

That Delicious Well Water —
Too Bad It May Be Radioactive

Much of the bedrock of Maine is granite, that beautiful rock which, sculpted into hills by the glaciers, provides much of Mount Desert Island's charm.

Recent scientific studies indicate that wells drilled into granite — many in Maine are — may be providing the people who drink water from them with dangerous doses of radioactive radon gas that results from the natural decay of uranium found in the granite.

Early results of one study by the state into links between radon from well water and the incidence of cancer "suggest we have something to look into," said Dr. Peter Rand, research chief at Portland's Maine Medical Center, in 1984.

The highest levels of radon in Maine have been found in the Sebago Lake, Georgetown and Bar Harbor areas. Some homes already have filters on their water pipes to take out the radon.

8 Industry

A Ralph Nader-sponsored book on Maine is entitled *The Paper Plantation*. The seven huge paper corporations are all headquartered out of state: International Paper, Boise Cascade, Georgia Pacific, etc. They own forty percent of the forest which covers nearly ninety percent of this most heavily timbered state. The woods products industry, the largest, employs forty thousand — a big number in a little over a million population. There are fourteen paper mills. Over forty percent of manufacturing income is from forest products.

Understandably, the paper companies have a colonial viewpoint. They historically have considered the state their private preserve. Land-use laws are barely enforced in their domain, the legislature crawls with their lobbyists, and they contribute heavily to the campaign treasuries of all the significant politicians. Taxes? The paper companies laugh scornfully at the idea that they should be taxed like everybody else. The state government collects the property taxes for the "unorganized territories" (where there is no municipal government), but the paper companies convinced the legislature to pass a law limiting the amount the state could take in taxes from this vast chunk of Maine to the cost of "services" — six small schools, etc. — received. As a result, the property-tax collection from the paper companies amounts to less than one percent of the state's total revenues. The companies even convinced the Maine Supreme Court to tell the legislature it didn't have much choice but to set up this bargain!

The companies have been accused by their critics of raping the forest: clear-cutting, not re-planting, and planning to move their operations to Alabama or Brazil after they have cut all the trees and written off their mills under the accelerated-depreciation tax schedule. They have recently started putting up for sale whole townships of cut-over land. A plane ride over the northern woods reduces Sierra Club members to tears. Even the companies admit that a shortage of wood is looming. Destroying the trees is one thing, but their praying-mantis-like harvesting machines pretty much destroy the earth as well.

The paper companies have also felt persecuted recently because of criticisms leveled at them for the spraying of enormous quantities of poisonous chemicals over Maine every year. They do this to keep the pests off the trees, but it doesn't work. In fact, the spraying seems to be prolonging the spruce budworm moth infestation. The dead trees produced by this infestation, ironically, are the excuse the companies use when justifying their heavy cutting practices.

The spraying program used to be financed by the taxpayers. Now the state simply administers it so the companies don't have to face liability for the numerous spraying accidents. If they did, they'd probably shut the program down as being too expensive.

Up on the Paper Plantation

Working in the woods, statistically one of the riskiest of jobs, is very poorly paid in this poorest of states. The companies hire loggers generally as independent contractors to get around such unpleasantries as health benefits and workmen's compensation. It also allows them to set the price — take it or leave it. To further keep the locals in line, the companies import grateful French Canadians who, coming from an even poorer land, are loyal to their employers.

However, occasionally the natives do get restless. On the famous warm night of August 17, 1977, not long after wood deliveries had been cut back by the St. Regis Paper Company, about forty Americans approached the twenty cabins of the St. Regis logging camp near First Machias Lake in eastern Maine. Telephone and power lines were cut. Windows were broken. Nineteen French loggers were driven away.

The leader of the protests during the past ten years has been the Maine Woodsmen's Association. It maintains that the French Canadian workers are being brought in illegally and keeps up a clamor about the over-cutting of the woods. The MWA began in 1975 with a strike that shut down the Diamond International mill in Old Town and reduced production at other mills. But the paper companies got a judge to lay down an injunction severely limiting picketing. Its effect was to stop the strike.

During the injunction proceeding, the governor, Independent James Longley, a millionaire insurance super-salesman, telephoned the judge to get him to hurry up so the strike would end. The judge told the lawyers involved that he had been "improperly" approached. Longley also threatened to bring in thousands of Canadians. The MWA said Longley made his fortune selling group insurance to the paper companies.

Calling this Scott Paper clearcut near Bingham a "Biomass Site" is like calling rape a biological experiment

At least Rumford lets you know the air is bad: Just look and smell

Breathe That Maine Air! (But Not Too Deeply)

The reputation Maine has for clean, bracing air has always seemed a bit strange to anyone living near the state's numerous paper mills or fish-processing plants. Strange, also, to anyone who reads the papers about how all the industrial wastes and byproducts of automobile exhaust poured into the air throughout the Northeast and Midwest are carried by the prevailing winds into Maine in the form of acid rain and ozone.

Acid rain has already wiped out, by rendering them as sour as vinegar, the fish life in a number of Maine ponds, and speculation abounds on what its long-term effect will be on Maine's forests. Ozone, which nineteenth-century tourists used to think was a good thing, is the major component of smog, which provides great Maine summer sunsets. It originates to a considerable extent as car and factory exhaust to the south and west of the state. Both Maine's pine trees and humans are sensitive to ozone. The pine trees have their needles die. The humans get eye irritations and have difficulty breathing. Although air pollution controls in recent years have generally lowered the levels of most pollutants, ozone is holding its own.

The paper mills produce sulfur dioxide, which has in the past been a major villain in some of the world's great air pollution disasters — the old, sick and very young gave out like fish on a dock. The paper companies have been forced to clean up their emissions, and supposedly SO^2 levels are not now hazardous to your health, but gawd does it — and other sulfurous chemicals in the air — smell!

Paper-mill towns — for instance, Jay and Lincoln — are burdened with another pollutant. In 1982 there were 152 violations throughout Maine of the state's air quality standards for "total suspended particulates," which means dirt and dust in the air from the mills as well as from construction sites, sawdust piles, automobile exhaust. Dust in the lungs may lead to shortness of breath, heart problems, emphysema, etc. Not just paper-mill towns are involved. Presque Isle's air has been getting dirtier in recent years from all the sanding done on the streets.

Other pollutants in Maine air, not counting miscellaneous smells from fish, manure, and so on, include carbon monoxide, lead, and nitrogen dioxide. Enjoy! Enjoy!

ACID RAIN

In the sixties, if you referred to "acid," people would have thought you were talking about psychedelics. But in the grimy, down-to-earth eighties, acid is more often

The Saco dump hazardous waste site. Industry claims that technology will come up with an antidote to this, called "Social Conscience," by the year 2025.

HAZARDOUS WASTE SITES IN MAINE

NOTE: If you can't go see one of these simply go down to your local garage whose leaking fuel tanks may be contaminating your water.

GRAY — McKin Company

WINTHROP — Winthrop-Savage landfill

SACO — Saco Tannery waste pits

AUGUSTA — O'Connor's junkyard

BAILEYVILLE — PCBs in a gravel pit

BUCKFIELD — Waste oil dump

There are seventy-two Environmental Protection Agency-listed potential hazardous waste disposal sites in Maine.

linked with senility than with mind expansion. Researchers have found that acid rain leaches aluminum out of the soil and this plentiful metal not only kills fish, other aquatic life and our lakes, it works its way via the food chain into the human brain, where too high a concentration of it apparently causes Alzheimer's Disease, otherwise known as premature senility. Right now only five percent of the population over sixty-five is afflicted with this disease, but if Midwest industries keep pumping their pollutants into the prevailing westerlies then maybe most of us in Maine can look foward to...ah...ah...what...well...ah...

Alzheimer's Disease may not be as awful as it sounds, however. So what if the memory is shot to hell? So what if the victim can no longer feed or clothe himself or herself? So what if he or she loses control over bodily functions? So what if he or she turns into aluminum foil? Mainers have always put up with adversity. Once again we'll prove...that...ah...ah...

TYPICAL LEGISLATIVE GIFT TO BIG BUSINESS PROVED UNNECESSARY THIS TIME

In 1978 Governor James Longley herded the legislators into a one-day special session to pass a $2.1-million income-tax abatement for Pratt & Whitney. It also applied to any other firm creating two hundred new jobs through at least a $5-million investment.

Longley told the legislators that unless they passed this tax break, Pratt & Whitney, the aircraft-engine-manufacturing division of United Technologies, would not locate a new plant in North Berwick.

Pressure for passage was intense. Longley flew legislative leaders to Pratt & Whitney headquarters in Connecticut. They came back true believers. Newspaper editorialists exulted over the benefits to Maine. The story was on the front pages for days.

Pratt & Whitney did go to North Berwick, but it never even took advantage of the famous tax break which bears its name until after newspaper reports noted this fact years later. Maybe they just forgot about the money they had squeezed from Maine taxpayers. After all, what's $2.1 million to United Technologies!

HE'S A BIW MAN*

(Dedicated to Union No. 6)

He taps rivets with bare hands
He brushes his teeth with asbestos
He eats sandwiches made of spam
He's a BIW MAN

He can sweep, wire and rig
He can weld better than anyone can
He builds destroyers bigger than big
He's a BIW MAN

He can read any blueprint
He can follow any plan
To obliterate the Commies
He's a BIW MAN

He builds guns, no butter
And anyone who is not a fan
He curses with a mutter
He's a BIW MAN

He's in the union, Number 6
And he always takes a stand
While the rest of Maine starves
He's a BIW MAN

BIGGER Defense Budgets are what he wants
More launches with the Navy Band
More and more money he flaunts
He's a BIW MAN

Whoever gets killed in the war
Fought with a BIW tincan
Doesn't bother him, that's sure
He's a BIW MAN

---

*BIW is the Bath Iron Works, Maine's largest employer. It makes ships — almost exclusively now for the Navy. The ultimate blue-collar employment in Maine is to work for BIW, where the wages, though modest by national standards, at least allow one to put a meal on the table, unlike Maine's many minimum-wage jobs.

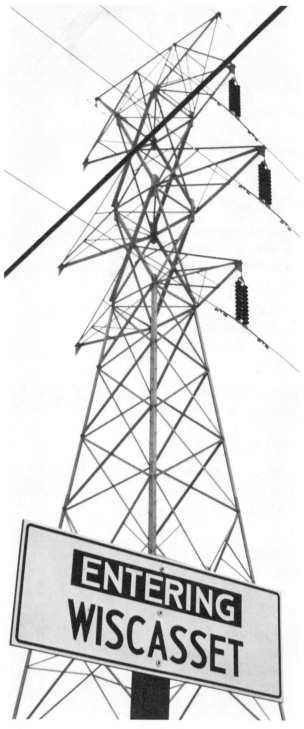

Maine people have had a love-hate relationship with nuclear power. At first they loved it because utility officials promised them electricity "too cheap to meter." Now, after Maine's only nuclear power plant, Maine Yankee at Wiscasset, has been on line for a dozen-plus years, a good proportion of Mainers hate it. Forty-four percent, according to the results of the second referendum that called for shutting down Maine Yankee, voted to shut it down. The plant, with its accidents, its unforeseen costs, and its ardent detractors and defenders, remains controversial.

From the
Uncensored Maine News Service

MAINE YANKEE UNVEILS NEW PLAN FOR SPENT FUEL RODS

WISCASSET, Maine — On the eve of the hearing before the Nuclear Regulatory Commission on its proposed expansion of its spent-fuel-rod storage capacity, Maine Yankee Atomic Power Company has changed the controversial waste-disposal design by adding a human dimension.

According to Maine Yankee spokesman Donald Frigue, the company has devised a use for the approximately 2,400 empty spaces between spent-fuel-rod assemblies.

"Conservation is a key concept at Maine Yankee," said Frigue at a hastily arranged news conference. "We hate to see those empty spaces go to waste. As a result, we have decided to fill them with Maine's antinuclear protestors."

The new plan alleviates the major objection that had been originally raised against the spent-fuel proposal, explained Frigue. "The dissident flesh, when packed between spent-fuel rods, will act as a buffer zone between rods and will thus prevent any overheating and meltdown or explosion by absorbing the excess heat of the rods. I don't know why we didn't think of it before."

Frigue was asked if Maine Yankee was certain the plan would work. He admitted that the company had tried it out on some antinuclear activists last month.

"We packed them in a spent-fuel rack for twenty-four hours and when we let them out they were completely changed. All of their hair had fallen out. Their gums had turned green. They needed wheelchairs to get around. But, best of all, their attitudes had turned around. They no longer mouthed antinuclear propaganda. Instead, we had a hard time distinguishing what they were saying from our publicity brochures."

Frigue was also asked if he anticipated any objections to the plan at tomorrow's hearing before the Nuclear Regulatory Commission. "Not really," he said. "The NRC recognizes the gravity of the situation and have told us in private, over cocktails and lobsters, that they are delighted by the originality of our plan. They will probably recommend its adoption by other nuclear power plants around the country."

THE NUCLEAR MAINE THAT NEVER WAS

The following is an abridged list of nuclear reactors that have been proposed for Maine; imagine what the landscape would be like if they had been built.

1. *Owl's Head*: Proposed site for a nuclear power plant by Public Power of Maine, a citizens' group that generated a lot of talk, but not much heat. Central Maine Power essentially killed the Owl's Head proposal by announcing plans for Maine Yankee in 1966. The better-organized and -financed CMP finessed their nuclear reactor plan through the legislature and nuclear bureaucracy before Public Power could do the same with theirs.

2. *Trenton:* TEPCO, an out-of-state company, proposed that a combination aluminum smelter/ nuclear reactor be located across the water from Acadia National Park. A special Trenton referendum in 1969 defeated the plan and drove TEPCO out of town. After that, they tried to get their plant built in a number of other Maine towns, but met resistance everywhere, and were last heard from in Berlin, New Hampshire.

3. *Sears Island:* First proposed by CMP in 1974 in the days when it looked like there was no end to the number of nuclear power plants they would build in Maine, Searsport residents overwhelmingly *approved* the plant in a nonbinding referendum in 1975, and it looked like it was going to fly until an earthquake fault was discovered on the site.

4. *Richmond:* CMP's second choice after the Sears Island disappointment, scheduled to come on line in the 1990s. This plant on the Kennebec River would have had Three-Mile-Island-type cooling towers. The plan was put on hold in 1977 when the state legislature passed a moratorium on any new nuclear power plant construction in Maine.

5. *York:* Public Service of New Hampshire proposed moving the Seabrook nuclear reactor across the border to York in a desperate attempt to diffuse protests against Seabrook by Mainers. Mostly just a smokescreen.

6. *Southern Maine coast:* Proposed as "ideal" location for a nuclear-power complex by a 1976 Nuclear Regulatory Commission report. Complex would consist of up to twenty reactors and produce thirty times more power than Maine Yankee. Construction would take fifteen to twenty years and large work crews "could contribute significantly to a more stable population."

7. *Wiscasset:* The U.S. Department of Energy released a plan in 1980 that called for building a "super nuclear park" of four breeder reactors at the Maine Yankee site by the year 2025. "If you need more nuclear power, expand the existing sites — don't dirty up the new ones," explained Brian Grimes of the Nuclear Regulatory Commission. This report is filed under "Elephants, White," but may be heard from again.

Tom Jones

Fishermen look for giant mutant lobsters in the waters near Maine Yankee. Three men died when huge claws plucked them from their boats, it has been rumored

Mark Melnicove

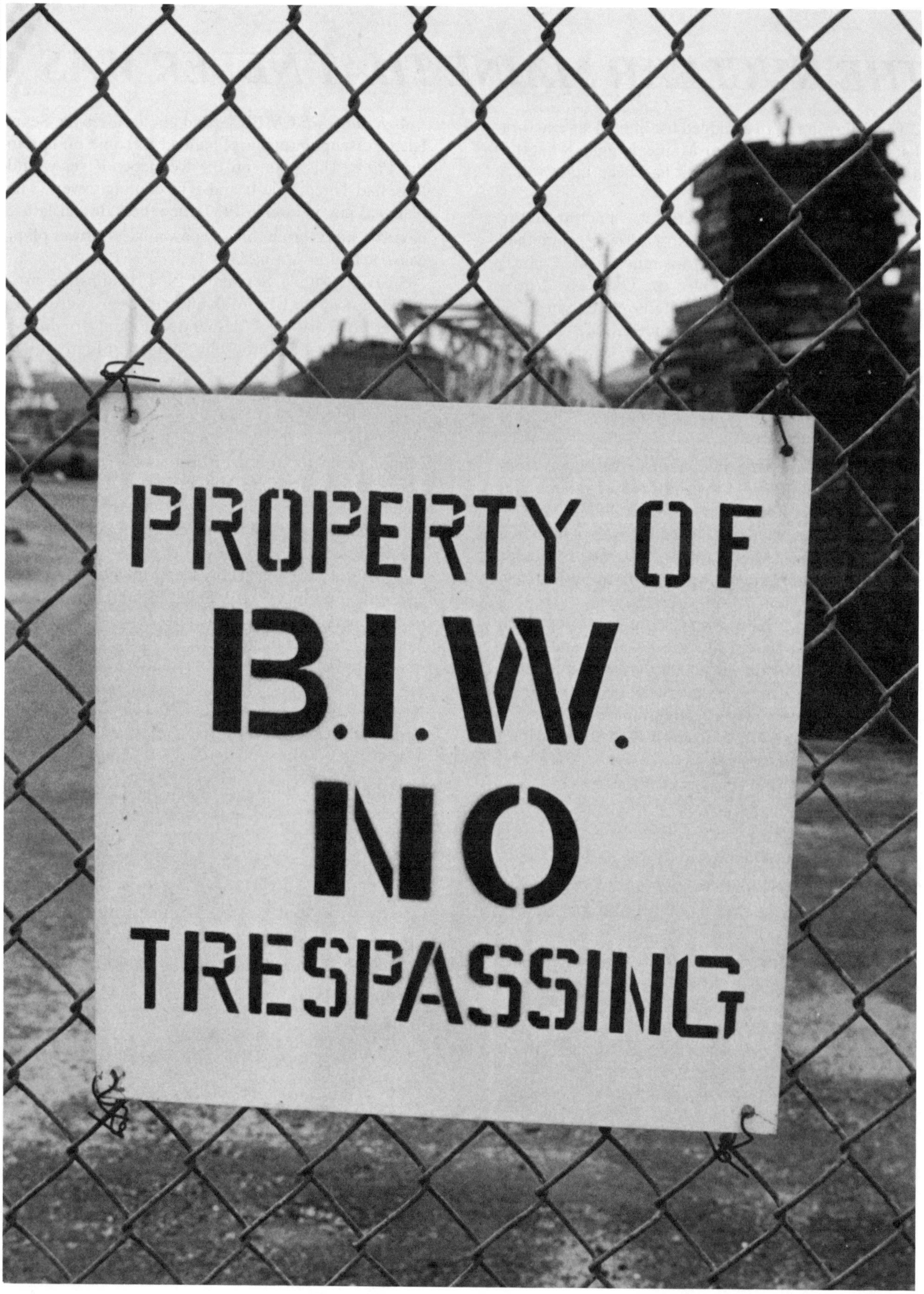

9 *Who Owns Maine?*

MAJOR LANDOWNERS IN MAINE

1. The Big Seven paper companies	6,764,396 acres	34.2%
2. Forest products industry (not including the Big Seven)	1,173,190 acres	5.9%
3. Out-of-state timberland owners & individual woodlot owners	7,319,300 acres	37.0%
4. Non-forest-based corporations that own land in the Maine woods	408,500 acres	2.1%
5. State of Maine	700,000 acres (est.)	3.5%
6. Federal government	138,132 acres	0.7%
7. Local governments	100,000 acres (est.)	0.5%
8. Indians	300,000 acres (est.)	1.5%
9. Farms (not including woodlands)	1,468,674 acres	7.4%
10. Industrial facilities	200,000 acres (est.)	1.0%
11. Commercial facilities	400,000 acres (est.)	2.0%
12. Roads, railroads, electrical transmission lines	200,000 acres (est.)	1.0%
13. Everyone else	624,908 acres (est.)	3.2%
TOTAL	19,797,100	100.0%

THE BIG 7

Name of Company	Headquarters	No. of Vice-Presidents	No. of pulp & paper mill locations	No. of acres owned in Maine
1. Great Northern Paper Co.	Stamford, CT	4	6 (2 in Maine)	2,100,000
2. International Paper Co.	New York, NY	24	14 (1 in Maine)	1,101,137
3. Scott Paper Co.	Philadelphia, PA	15	16 (3 in Maine)	860,000
4. Diamond International Corporation	New York, NY	12	9 (0 in Maine)	801,000
5. St. Regis Corporation	New York, NY	23	16 (1 in Maine)	760,000
6. Boise Cascade Paper Group	Boise, ID	26	19 (1 in Maine)	598,259
7. Georgia-Pacific Corporation	Atlanta, GA	25	19 (1 in Maine)	544,000
		129	99 (9 in Maine)	6,764,396

1. THE BIG SEVEN

Ninety percent of Maine's 19,797,100 acres are covered with trees. Ninety-five percent of these trees are classified as commercial forest; the Big Seven own forty percent of it. The bulk of Maine's wood-cutting operations takes place in the Unorganized Territory (8,269,733 acres or forty-one percent of Maine). The Big Seven own fifty-nine percent of the Unorganized Territory.

Great Northern Paper Co. is Maine's largest landowner; it owns eleven percent of the state. Probably no other corporation in the country owns as much of one state as Great Northern owns of Maine. Number two on the Big Seven list, International Paper Co., is the "largest industrial landowner in North America" — more than seven million acres of timberland are under its control.

DID YOU KNOW? DO YOU CARE?

...that only a half cord of new woods growth occurs per acre per year...that 1980 timber operations in Maine produced 782 million cords of softwood, 140.9 million cords of hardwood lumber and 3.4 million cords of pulpwood...that, according to the Paper Industry Information Office, one cord of wood will yield 7,500,000 toothpicks.

DID YOU KNOW? DO YOU CARE?

...that twenty to fifty million gallons of water flow through each of Maine's largest paper mills each day?...that Americans consume 650 pounds of paper per person per year?...that next to mining, woods work is the most dangerous occupation in America?...that anywhere from one million to three million acres of the Maine woods has been clear-cut in recent years?...that it doesn't pay to replant the Maine woods?

2. THE REST OF THE FOREST PRODUCTS INDUSTRY:

The Big Seven combined with the rest of the forest products industry (manufacturers of paper, wood, toothpicks, waferboard, tongue depressors, shingles, lobster traps, matches, clothespins, barrels, wooden toys, etc.) own forty-seven percent of Maine's commercial forest acreage. According to the U.S. Forest Service, "in no other state does industry ownership account for such a high percentage of forest land." The forest products industry has access to nearly every tree in the state. Independent woodsmen have no other market for the wood they cut except for Maine (and Canadian) mills. In essence, then, the forest products industry owns the entire Maine woods.

3. OUT-OF-STATE TIMBERLAND OWNERS AND INDIVIDUAL WOODLOT OWNERS:
Out-of-state timberland ownership of the Maine woods is big business. Our conservative estimate is that big timberland corporations like Irving Pulp & Paper, Pingree Associates, J.M. Huber Corp. G.P. Webber, E.G. Dunn Heirs, Baskahegan and Coburn Lands Trust own at least fifty percent of the 7,319,300 acres listed under number three. The remaining fifty percent is owned by "100,000 individuals" (according to the U.S. Forest Service).

4. NON-FOREST-BASED CORPORATIONS THAT OWN LAND IN THE MAINE WOODS:
The figure listed under number four comes from a U.S. Forest Service report for 1971. These corporations are defined as "businesses such as recreation industries, ski areas, boys' and girls' camps; power companies, water districts, etc."

5. STATE LANDS:
The state of Maine once owned eight million acres of public land, but gave away or sold nearly all of it for pennies an acre during the fifty-plus years following statehood in 1820. Approximately eighty to ninety percent of this land is owned, today, by some twenty out-of-state corporations, including the Big Seven.

In the nineteenth-century the state couldn't get rid of its eight million acres fast enough; it was only during the twentieth century that a few individuals began to be interested in getting some of it back. Former Governor Percival Baxter is responsible for buying, with his own money (because the state legislature was intimidated by the paper companies), 200,000 acres of the park now named after him that surrounds Mount Katahdin. Other state parks and memorials (such as the Allagash Wilderness Waterway and Fort Popham) account for another 67,173 acres of state land. In addition, Inland Fisheries and Wildlife owns 48,113 acres of hatcheries, game management areas and eider nesting islands throughout the state.

The big land story during recent years has been the public lots controversy. Soon after statehood, public lots of one thousand acres were reserved by the state in each twenty-three-thousand-acre township of the Unorganized Territory. These lots were set aside to provide support for public schools and churches when the Unorganized Territory was settled. But the settlers never came; northern Maine didn't become the thriving metropolis our ancestors in state government envisioned it would be.

Around 1850, the state began to sell the cutting rights to these public lots, but, through so-called administrative neglect, it was assumed that not only the cutting rights but also the ownership of these lands had been sold to private entrepreneurs. It wasn't until 1972 that a series of newspaper articles in the *Maine Sunday Telegram* by

BIGGEST FIVE PROPERTIES OWNED BY THE FEDERAL GOVERNMENT IN MAINE

Name of Facility	Agency	Township or area	Year Acquired	Acreage
1. White Mountain National Forest	U.S. Forest Service	Western Maine	1918	47,283.5
2. Acadia National Park	National Park Service	Mt. Desert Island	1916	34,427.5
3. Moosehorn National Wildlife Refuge	Fish & Wildlife	Baring & Cobscook Bay	1936	22,655.6
4. Loring Air Force Base	Air Force	Limestone	1947	9,374.0
5. Northeast Forest Experimental Station	U.S. Forest Service	Orono	1937	3,694

Source: General Services Administration

reporter Bob Cummings brought to light the fact that the state still owned these lands. The timber and grass rights sold to various landowners during the nineteenth century, Cummings pointed out, covered the timber standing at the time of the sale and not the trees grown and harvested on them since. This conclusion was contested by some of the big landowners in court, but the state finally won the seven-year judicial battle and now finds itself with 400,000 acres it had forgotten about.

The public lots are managed by the Bureau of Public Lands. "Most of the bureau's $665,000 annual budget is raised from the sale of timber," writes Cummings in a 1983 newspaper article, "and most of that is plowed back into planning for more timber harvesting. Public recreation on the 400,000 acres was allotted just $30,000, or about seven cents an acre (during 1982)." The state is so strapped for money that it can't even afford to put up signs in the public lots to tell tourists where they are. Cummings describes campsites in the spectacular Mahoosuc mountains as nothing short of "wilderness slums."

Is it any wonder, then, that when we attempted to get an accurate figure of the total amount of land owned by the state of Maine, the state was unable to help us? We were told the state didn't have the money necessary to keep track of all its land. We were told it was not a question that had to be answered in order for the government to function. The seven hundred thousand acres we list under number 5, therefore, is the amount we were able to verify — there is undoubtedly more.

6. FEDERAL GOVERNMENT: When you add it all up — dollars for defense, veterans benefits, social security, food stamps, AFDC, grants to state and local governments and nonprofit organizations, tax breaks, dollars for education and media, etc. — Uncle Sam controls a larger part of the Maine economy than any other business. Most amazing about the federal government's grip on the Maine economy, however, is that it accomplishes this extraordinary feat even though it owns only 0.7 percent of Maine. Just think how much more powerful it would be if it owned more!

The federal government owns thirty-one percent of the United States. It owns eighty-four percent of Alaska. Only Iowa (0.63 percent) and Connecticut (0.317 percent) rank lower than Maine in percentage of state land owned by Uncle Sam.

7. LOCAL GOVERNMENTS: One hundred thousand acres is our conservative guess for the number of acres owned by counties, cities, townships and plantations.

8. INDIANS: Maine Indians weep when they see what has happened to their land. The concept of private property is not native with them; it was brought to Maine almost four hundred years ago by European settlers. Thanks to the 1980 Land Claims Settlement, the Indians now own a piece of the pie (three hundred thousand acres) but it is a very small piece compared to what used to be theirs. They are trying to make money off their land just like everyone else, mostly through logging operations. The most profitable venture for them thus far seems to be a blueberry operation owned by the Passamaquoddys in Washington County, near the Over-the-Horizon radar receiver.

on Indian Island

9. FARMS: Farmland acreage is declining. It has dropped from 4.5 million to 1.5 million acres since 1945. The increase in Maine forest land since then is due to abandoned agricultural lands being taken over by trees.

Maine Farms: Who Owns Them? (1982)

Individual or family	90.0%
Partnership	5.5%
Corporation	4.0 %
Other	0.5%
	100.0%

49.5 percent of Maine farms sold less than $5,000 worth of agricultural products in 1982.

Source: U.S. Dept. of Agriculture

10. INDUSTRIAL FACILITIES: (See estimate.)

11. COMMERCIAL FACILITIES: (See estimate.)

12. ROADS, ETC.: Maine has thirty-two thousand miles of road, over four thousand miles of electric transmission lines and 2,249 miles of railroad crisscrossing the state. No one has accurate figures on how much land this takes up. The Department of Transportation refuses to even guess; two hundred thousand acres, a mere one percent of the state, seemed conservative enough. It could be much higher.

13. EVERYONE ELSE: 624,908 acres (or about ½ acre per Mainer) is what's left for you and me when everything else is subtracted. It's not a whole lot of land, but it'll have to do.

LAST WORDS: Maine possibly holds the dubious distinction of having more of its private land owned by out-of-staters than any other state. Our conservative estimate puts the figure at three-quarters. In other words, Maine is indeed a colony — literally.

Top Twenty Manufacturers By Size, Maine, 1982

	Number of Workers	Percent of Total
TOTAL, MANUFACTURING EMPLOYMENT	109,584	100.0%
TOTAL, TOP TWENTY MANUFACTURERS	38,968	35.6
Employers with over 3,000 Workers	14,610	13.3
Bath Iron Works*		
Chesebrough-Ponds, Inc.*		
Great Northern Paper*		
Employers with 1,500 to 2,999 Workers	11,841	10.8
Boise-Cascade Paper Co.*		
Dexter Shoe Co.		
Diamond International*		
International Paper Co.*		
Keyes Fiber*		
Scott Paper Co.*		
Employers with 1,200 to 1,499 Workers	3,871	3.5
Fairchild Camera & Instrument*		
St. Regis Paper Co.*		
Warnaco*		
Employers with 1,000 to 1,199 Workers	8,646	7.9
Forster Manufacturing		
Fraser Paper Co.*		
Georgia-Pacific Corp.*		
GTE Sylvania*		
Guilford Industries*		
NIKE, Inc.*		
Sprague Electric*		
United Technologies*		

absentee (out-of-state) owned

Source: Maine Department of Labor, Bureau of Labor Standards, Research & Statistics Division

10 Government

GENESIS

In the beginning, Muskie created the heaven and the earth. And Muskie said, "Let there be Maine," and there was Maine. And Muskie saw Maine, that it was good: and Muskie divided Maine from the other forty-nine states. And Muskie called Maine "Vacationland," and everyone else "tourists." And that was the end of the first day.

And Muskie said, "Let there be a firmament in the midst of the waters, and let it divide the Republicans from the Democrats." And Muskie made the firmament, and it was so. And Muskie called the firmament "the two-party system." And that was the end of the second day.

And Muskie said, "Let the waters under heaven be gathered together unto one place, and let the dry land appear": and it was so. And Muskie called the dry land Augusta; and the gathering together of the waters he called the Kennebec River: and Muskie became Governor there. And Muskie said, "Let the earth bring forth grass and the herbe yielding seed, and let the Department of Transportation come in and pave it all over." And it was so. And the earth brought forth grass and I-95 brought forth more tourists. And it was good. And that was the end of the third day.

And Muskie made two great lights; the greater light to rule the day, he called the Sun, and the lesser light to rule the night, he called L.L. Bean's. And Freeport, Maine, became the fashion capital of the world. And that was the end of the fourth day.

And Muskie said, "Let the waters bring forth abundantly the moving creatures that hath life, and let the Shaw's and Hannaford Brothers supermarket chains have a monopoly on that life." And Muskie blessed them, saying, "Be fruitful and multiply and put the corner stores out of business." And it was so. And that was the end of the fifth day.

And Muskie said, "Let the earth bring forth more living creatures since so many others are on the endangered species list," and it was so. And Muskie made trees just like the tourists wanted them, but Muskie couldn't figure out how to get rid of the polluters. So he had a lot of new laws passed, but still the polluters wouldn't go away. So, when he became Senator, he created the Environmental Protection Agency, and from that day on he didn't have to think about industrial polluters anymore.

And Muskie said, "I can't go on like this forever, let me make a man in my own image, after my own likeness: and let him have dominion over Maine." So Muskie created George Mitchell in his own image. And Mitchell said, "I will do everything Muskie tells me and go to heaven afterwards." And Muskie heard this and blessed George Mitchell, saying, "Behold, I have given you the coast and most of it is private, and I have given you the rivers, and most of them are dammed, and at Bar Harbor I have given you scientists to genetically alter things if they don't go as planned." And it was so. And Muskie saw everything he had made and was proud. And he made George Mitchell a U.S. Senator, and he put on his tuxedo and went out on the town to celebrate. And that was the end of the sixth day.

And on the seventh day Muskie had a hangover and didn't get out of bed. And he decided he enjoyed not messing around with Maine anymore. And so he blessed the seventh day, and sanctified it; and then he went back to sleep.

Former State Rep. Stanley "Tuffy" Laffin once told the legislature, in his fight against the "gay rights" bill, that if any lesbian ever spent a night with him she wouldn't be a lesbian any more. Laffin was also big on reinstating the death penalty.

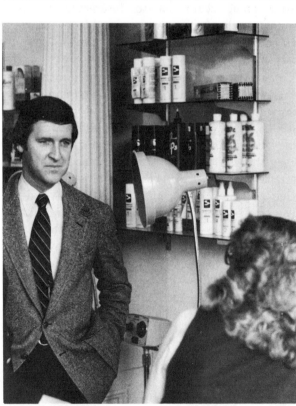

Many people credit Senator Bill Cohen's political success to his hairspray. Here he is shown consulting with a beautician.

An Uncensored Bill Cohen Poem

As most people in Maine know, popular U.S. Senator Bill Cohen is a poet. At least, he had a book of poems, *Of Sons and Seasons*, published by a major New York publisher...and, hey, it's not that easy to have done even if you're a famous and influential U.S. Senator! Some of the critics thought his poems were sentimental, but Maine people thought there was nothing wrong in writing about babies, dogs, Mom, Republicans, apple pie, etc. Just to prove that Bill Cohen isn't sentimental, the *Uncensored Guide* is privileged to publish for the first time a poem left out of his book. Somehow, his editors felt it didn't quite fit with the subject matter of *Sons and Seasons*, although the style and grace of language is similar.

TO THE THIEF IN THE NIGHT WHO STOLE MY WAR CHEST AND SPENT IT ALL ON FLOWERS

So quick to steal the money
given to my re-election campaign
by the nation's largest defense contractors,
you gathered up my dollars
without my permission
and stuffed them hurriedly
into your rainbow-colored bag.

And when you visited
all the florist shops
in Maine,
my dollars poured out of your bag
and into the cash registers,
and you mailed the purchased posies
to every registered voter
in the state
in lieu of my campaign literature!

To you who would
turn me into a buffoon
and pretend to all
that I am a pansy:
Beware. You would be better off
if you had my dollars still —
they would not have wilted
in the face of Soviet aggression!
Your flowers do!

PAPER-COMPANY FREEBEES:
A FRINGE BENEFIT FOR LEGISLATORS

For years selected legislators have been going on annual entertainment and deer-hunting junkets to paper-company lodges in the northern woods. "We go to sport a little," one legislator said when asked about the trip he used to take each year to hunt from International Paper's lodge on Fourth Musquacook Lake.

The legislators IP often invited were important to their concerns such as Senator James McBreairty, a Caribou Republican who, until the Democrats took over the State Senate, was chair of the energy and natural resources committee.

The legislators involved see nothing wrong in this practice. It doesn't even get in the way of the vigorous defense they make of paper-company policies, for which Sen. McBreairty is perhaps most vigorous. Even though the Maine press chooses to ignore the trips, their details are spread out in the financial reports required of all lobbyists in Maine.

The laws of Maine declare that a legislative "conflict of interest shall include...where a legislator...accepts gifts, other than campaign contributions duly recorded as required by law, from persons affected by legislation."

The law says that a legislator is not supposed to vote on legislation where he has a conflict of interest. When the legislator does vote, however, the law only provides that someone may complain to the Commission on Governmental Ethics and Election Practices. If the commission decides a conflict of interest has occured, then it reports to the legislature, which may or may not censure the legislator.

When the trips were brought to the attention of an assistant attorney general assigned to the secretary of state's office and the former staff person of the governmental ethics commission, he showed little interest in pursuing the matter. "It's been going on for a long time," he said. "It's always been looked at as something legislators do to inform themselves."

Guy Gannett Newspapers

Legislators consulting with lobbyists beneath the rotunda of the Capitol

David Emery Is Not as Dumb as You Think!

David Emery, the former Republican U.S. congressman who lost in his bid to take the U.S. Senate seat away from George Mitchell in 1982, is now second in command at the U.S. Arms Control and Disarmament Agency. This development has led many Maine Democrats and Independents to wish that they had voted for Emery for the U.S. Senate, where, if elected, he potentially would be less dangerous than in his current position. Their concerns stem from Emery's alleged lack of smarts. However, to reassure the Maine population that David Emery is not as dumb as they think, we present these two illustrations.

Guy Gannett Newspapers

David Emery proves he can receive an honorary degree and stand up at the same time

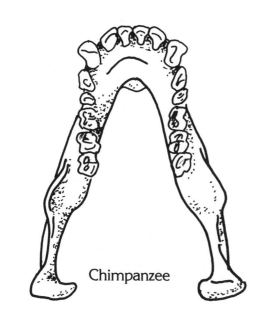

Chimpanzee

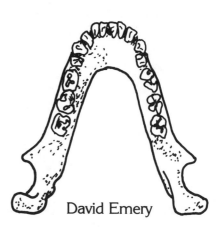

David Emery

Dental records prove that David Emery is no chimpanzee

The Morning After (the MX Vote)

The Scene: Congressman Jockstrap and Congresswoman Snowball are having breakfast together in her Washington apartment. It is the morning after the vote in the House on whether to fund the MX missile.

JOCKSTRAP: Gee, you make really good pancakes. With all the time you spend on clothes, how did you ever learn to cook so well?

SNOWBALL: (Ignoring the question.) Well, you don't exactly skimp on the suits. I've heard Democrats call you a clothes horse.

JOCKSTRAP: (Laughs) O hell, in Maine if you have an extra shirt they call you a clothes horse! (They both laugh)...Mind passing me the butter?

SNOWBALL: Sorry, we're all out. Like some guns instead?

JOCKSTRAP: (Looking disgruntled) I can tell what's on your mind this morning.

SNOWBALL: (Archly) Well, at least I didn't waffle all over the place about my vote! Honestly, you can't be firm about anything!

JOCKSTRAP: Well, at least we're on the good side of Reagan now, even if it'll cost us votes back home.

SNOWBALL: Oh, I don't think the people in Maine pay any attention to our votes. All we have to do is

U.S. Rep. Olympia Snowe is one of Washington's best-dressed women

Bangor Daily News

U.S. Rep. John McKernan is a well-known basketball and tennis player and all-around "jockstrap"

smile and look pretty. Anyway, we support the Freeze, don't we?

JOCKSTRAP: Yeah, but those Freeze people think it's inconsistent to support the Freeze *and* the MX...and Reagan thinks it's inconsistent, too, from the opposite view. Even after this vote I'm worried that he won't give us the military contracts we're after for Maine because we're not consistent in his eyes.

SNOWBALL: God! Doesn't anybody understand that they can't expect you to be consistent if you want to be re-elected...They don't understand what this is all about!

JOCKSTRAP: Yeah, and neither of us knew this was going to be so serious down here, with all the studying and hard work.

SNOWBALL: (Taking his hand across the sausage) Well, we do manage to have some fun, don't we?

JOCKSTRAP: Yeah, until we have to go back to Maine.

The New York Times

Edmund Muskie in New Hampshire in 1972. His dandruff problem finally knocked him out of the presidential race

Maine's Ugliest U.S. Senator

George Mitchell, unlike U.S. Sen. Bill Cohen and most other politicians these days, did not get elected on his looks, although this is not sure because his opponent in the last election was David Emery. In any case, Maine people have been concerned for some time that George Mitchell does not meet the standard of beauty set by Cohen and our two U.S. representatives, Olympia Snowe and John "Jock" McKernan. In order to help out the plastic surgeon that Mitchell is being urged to consult, we present this critique of his face:

Bangor Daily News

hair too thin and short

needs contact lenses

eliminate ears entirely

eliminate half of nose

more rouge on cheeks

cap all teeth

remove half of jaw

new skin

11 *A Maine Pestiary*

"Man's a lazy animal — pesticides help us get the most for our money."
James F. Dill, Pest Management Specialist,
Cooperative Extension Service, UMO

Bangor Daily News

Spruce-budworm spraying

A is for APPLE. It used to be good to eat. Especially a Maine apple. It is sprayed with more pesticides per acre than any other food in Maine. You had better peel it, although that won't help much. Some of those pesticides are:

— *Ammate:* also sprayed on poison ivy (herbicide)
* — *Benlate:* also sprayed on blueberries (fungicide)
* — *Captan:* also sprayed in greenhouses (fungicide)
— *Casoron:* also sprayed in nurseries (herbicide)
* — *Cyprex:* also sprayed on strawberries (fungicide)
* — *DiFolatan:* also sprayed on potatoes (fungicide)
* — *Dowpon:* also sprayed on potatoes (herbicide)
— *Ethion:* also sprayed on ornamental crops (insecticide-acaricide)
* — *Guthion:* also sprayed on blueberries (insecticide)
* — *Imidan:* also sprayed on potatoes (insecticide)
* — *Karmex:* also sprayed on blueberries (herbicide)
* — *Kelthane:* also sprayed in greenhouses (acaricide)
* — *Lannate:* also sprayed on corn (insecticide)
* — *Manzate:* also sprayed on potatoes (fungicide)
* — *Malathion:* also sprayed on highways (insecticide)
* — *Methoxychlor:* also sprayed on potatoes (insecticide)
* — *Niacide:* also sprayed on pears (fungicide)
— *Paraquat:* also sprayed on marijuana (herbicide)
* — *Plictran:* also sprayed on gardens (acaricide)
* — *Polyram:* also sprayed on potatoes (fungicide)
* — *Princep:* also sprayed on highways (herbicide)
* — *Round-up:* also sprayed on hardwoods (herbicide)
* — *Sinbar:* also sprayed on blueberries (herbicide)
* — *Systox:* also sprayed on potatoes (insecticide-acaricide)
* — *Thiodan:* also sprayed on potatoes (insecticide, acaricide)
* — *2,4-D:* also sprayed on highways (herbicide)
* — *Vendex:* also sprayed in greenhouses (acaricide)

A is also for AERIAL SPRAYING. Those pesticides marked * are sprayed from airplanes and helicopters. Often they drift farther than they are supposed to. Spruce budworm pesticides sprayed in Maine have been picked up as far as a hundred miles away from their point of origin. When the forests are sprayed, it may mean the whole state is being sprayed. *WARNING:* Don't breathe.

B is for the BROWNING of Maine roadsides. Browning is a technique used by the Department of Transportation to vary the scenery along the roads. One summer, tourists delight in a profusion of wildflowers and attractive shrubs. Returning to the same spots next year they are surprised to find highway weed killers have substantially altered their Vacationland experience. The tourist is forced to sit back and try to enjoy the many lethal shades of brown as best he can. No refunds available.

B is also for BANNED PESTICIDES. Hundreds of the pesticides thought safe yesterday are no longer considered safe today, and have been banned by the Environmental Protection Agency or restricted from use by the Maine State Board of Pesticides Control. Unfortunately, a lot of these pesticides (with names such as DDT, Endrin and Toxaphene) are collecting dust in Maine's barns, cellars, back sheds, fields and streams. Many are also leaking from their containers, if they are in containers. Many are used or dumped illegally. Hardly anyone ever gets caught.

C is for CAPTAN, the "pink stuff that gets all over your fingers when you plant vegetable seeds." It is thought to cause genetic damage and birth defects.

D is for DDT, "the atomic bomb of the insect world." For over twenty years after World War II it was everybody's favorite pesticide and was used extensively, with little precaution, indoors and out. Ants, bedbugs, birds, carpet beetles, cockroaches, firebrats, fleas, flies, fish, hornets, lice, mosquitos, silverfish, termites, ticks, wasps, hornets, mother's milk...not much was really sacred. DDT was the first pesticide tried against the spruce budworm. From 1954-1967 over one million pounds of it was dropped on the Maine woods in the futile attempt to eradicate the pest. Since then at least seven other pesticides have been used against it. RESULT: The budworm has lost a few battles but is winning the war.

E is for EVERYDAY MAINE CONSUMERS. Two-thirds of them claim to use insect repellent.

F is for FURADAN. Thousands of pounds a year are applied to field corn in Maine. It is made by Mobay Chemical Corporation (owned by Bayer Aspirin). Aspirin is what the farmer takes if he accidentally puts it in the wrong place. Symptoms of Furadan poisoning include lacrimation (abnormal and excessive crying), flaccidity (muscular weakness), tremors (a feeling of uncertainty and insecurity), vertigo (a dizzy confused state of mind), and dyspnea (shortness of breath). Too much Furadan can lead to convulsions and death by asphyxiation. Some believe the chemical companies secretly spray Furadan on legislators when they are considering bills to restrict chemical use. They demonstrate many of the above symptoms.

G is for GUTHION, very popular in Maine. It can make people sick and may cause birth defects. Less than a teaspoon of pure Guthion spilled on your skin would probably kill you. It was developed during World War II by the Nazis for use as a nerve gas. It is outlawed for use in warfare by the Geneva Convention. When asked to comment on the statement that Guthion "penetrates the skin of blueberries and other fruits, and is not, therefore, removed by washing," a Pesticides Control Board staffer said: "I suspect some gets through. If someone wants to make sure he doesn't have Guthion on his berries he should grow them himself."

H is for HEPTACHLOR. Like every other pesticide, it can kill more than two birds with one stone. Formerly used to rid your house of termites, it had the added plus of causing cancer and liver disorders in bothersome mice.

I is for INSPECTORS. The State Board of Pesticides Control can only afford to hire two field inspectors. An equivalent absurdity would be if there were only two game wardens in the state (there are 120).

J is for JUSTICE. Only two inspectors for a thirty-three-thousand-square-mile state means that the vast bulk of pesticide-law violations and the vast majority of health and environmental harm resulting from the spraying of pesticides goes undetected.

K is for CAMP KEYES, headquarters of the Maine National Guard in Augusta. It was used for pesticide storage until closed in 1980, leaving Maine with no state-approved dump (today the situation remains the same). The best the Board of Pesticides Control can do is wait until they buy an "obsolete pesticides recovery vehicle" and get it licensed. Then they will come pick up our trash. But where will they take it? In 1980, only two high-incineration dumps in the U.S. could be found without ties to organized crime or records of environmental violations, a state official was quoted as saying.

L is for LABOR, MIGRANT. They are the front line, the ones to bear the brunt of the sprays.

> **L** is also for LEBANON, a town in southwestern Maine. In 1983 it became the first town in Maine to outlaw the spraying of pesticides on utility right-of-ways and roads. Lebanon is substituting manual labor for pesticides, putting people to work instead of putting people out of work! A novel idea.

> **L** is also for LINDANE, the active ingredient in head-lice shampoos. It is also used on ornamental plants and as a treatment for some garden seeds. The medical advisory committee to the Pesticides Control Board ranks pesticides on a scale of one to three, with three being the most dangerous. Lindane gets a three for causing reproduction problems and for persistence in the environment, and "either a two or three" as a potential cause of cancer. It hardly seems worth nit-picking about.

THE AMAZING TEMIK

...Over 100 Maine wells have been found thus far to be contaminated with TEMIK.

...A quarter of a million pounds of TEMIK are purchased each year in Maine.

...Has not yet contaminated water supplies in Presque Isle, Ft. Fairfield and Houlton, but Ft. Fairfield's intricate system of wells and surface waters is a source of concern.

...Has been used in Maine since 1974.

...Growers apply it in granular form "since a drop or two of liquid TEMIK on the skin would be fatal."

...Called a systemic insecticide because it is "taken up by the roots and distributed throughout the entire plant system, and remains in all tissues of the plant, including the tubers, during much or all of the growing season. TEMIK is ready to kill any insect as soon as it begins to feed on any part of the plant."

...Described as "necessary" and "the only product that can do the job" by potato growers.

...Using their 0 (lowest) to 3 (highest) rating system, the Board of Pesticides Control came up with these numbers on TEMIK: *Toxicity* — 3; *Persistence in water* — 3; *Persistence in soil* — 2 or 3; *Mutagen* — 1; *Cause of cancer and birth defects* — 1.

...Department of Environmental Protection (DEP) regulations state that "all ground-water contamination by any synthetic is a violation," but they have chosen not to enforce the regulation in regard to TEMIK in spite of the fact that fifty-seven of the first 101 Maine wells that were sampled were contaminated with TEMIK.

...Residues of TEMIK were found on Maine potatoes during the winter of 1982 by the Food and Drug Administration. "Levels ranged as high as .35 parts per million, or 35 times as high as the critical EPA 'action level' for TEMIK in drinking water."

...New state regulations have established small fifty- to a hundred-foot buffer zones around wells where TEMIK is used, in spite of the fact that there are at least "eleven major variables affecting movement of pesticides in ground water," distance being only one of them.

...New labels provided by Union Carbide, the manufacturer, now require that TEMIK be applied after potato plants have emerged from the soil (four to six weeks after planting) instead of being planted with the seed stock as was done before. No one knows if this and other label restrictions will do any good, but it's cheaper in the short run than pulling TEMIK from the shelves.

...The contaminated Maine wells are not public info. Union Carbide and the University of Maine (they did the testing) are keeping the exact locations a secret. It is therefore impossible to report how many children, pregnant women and women who might get pregnant are currently drinking the contaminated water.

Bangor Daily News

This spruce-budworm-spray plane enjoyed a swim in the Allagash Wilderness Waterway

M is for MATACIL. In 1983 Number One pesticide in a long line of unsuccessful spruce budworm sprays. Its biggest-selling feature seemed to be that it was cheaper than all the rest. Early studies linked it with Reyes Syndrome. Pesticide spokesmen claim new Matacil formulas do not cause the syndrome. Time will tell. *WARNING:* You are a guinea pig.

N is for NO-SPRAY SIGNS. The Maine countryside is littered with these crudely lettered wooden and cardboard shields. These attempt to keep pesticides from drifting in where they aren't wanted. Good luck.

O is for OPEN-MOUTHED BOTTLES. In olden Maine, bottles were partly filled with a mixture of vinegar, molasses and water and hung in apple trees in June. These would catch coddling moths as they were laying their eggs. In another technique, pigs and chickens were positioned underneath the trees to eat the unwanted pests. There are no known cancers to have resulted from these methods.

> **O** is also for ORTHENE, used in the state-run spruce budworm program until it was discovered that the Illinois laboratory that did safety tests on it might have falsified the results.

P is for PERSISTENCE. Cold weather, acidic soil and dark days are features of life in Maine that we have come to know and love. Unfortunately, these are the ideal conditions for persistence of pesticides in our soil and water. This is not good because pesticides are dangerous until they break down. In spite of the danger of persistence, only a handful of pesticides used in Maine have ever been tested in the state before being put on the market.

R is for RIGHT-OF-WAYS. The electric utilities spray power-line right-of-ways. Telephone companies spray telephone-line right-of-ways. Oil companies spray oil-line right-of-ways. The Department of Transportation sprays the roads. "These right-of-ways pass close to people's homes at times. Children and pets can re-enter the area right after spraying and that may be too soon." (Robert Denny, director, Pesticides Control Board).

S is for SPRUCE BUDWORM, the largest aerial pesticide spray program in the United States. "Bring back the DDT," advises Joseph Lupsha, former state forester and former director of the Maine Forest Products Council. "Let's kill a few eagles and save forty million cords of wood," he says. Other budworm specialists disagree. They point out that no matter what pesticides have been used against the budworm, there have always been enough insects to survive and reproduce a full crop of tree-eating larvae next year.

The State of Maine has abandoned spraying the budworm on virtually all of its four hundred thousand acres of public lots because "we just can't afford it." Pretty soon the paper companies won't be able to afford it, either. These companies may pull out of Maine completely and flee to the South where efficient and aesthetically sterile tree farms seem like a bargain compared to the scraggly, budworm-infested Maine woods. "It is important that everyone understand that the cost of repeated spray protection exceeds the value of the trees," warns Jerry Williams of International Paper, one of Maine's top three sprayers. "We cannot justify protecting trees just to assure a future fiber supply," he adds.

The first recorded outbreak of the spruce budworm was in 1770. Other outbreaks occurred in 1806, 1878, 1910, and 1949. Only the most recent outbreak has been fought with pesticides (beginning in 1954 with DDT) and isn't over yet. After the publication of Rachel Carson's *Silent Spring* in 1962, DDT came under increasing attack. Its use was justified, however, in 1966 by Maine Forest Commissioner Austin Wilkins on the basis of a report compiled on bird populations during an earlier DDT program. Only after the 1966 spraying was done was it learned that this report was written by a high-school senior who was quoted as saying that he "hoped the report would remain in obscurity forever...this was the first effort I had ever made in the direction of scientific objectivity, and I feel that I was not entirely successful."

S is also for SEVIN, otherwise known as Carbaryl. Sevin was the Number One pesticide used against the spruce budworm, until it was withdrawn from use for being too dangerous to aquatic insects. It persists in Maine water up to eighteen months, which is three times longer than its manufacturer, Union Carbide, says it should. It is still the Number One pesticide ingredient in home-gardening applications. Anyone can buy and use it. It is deadly to bees who mistake it for pollen and feed it to their babies. It is thought to be a viral enhancer and has been linked with Reyes Syndrome. Some six million acres of Maine forestland was sprayed with it during the late 70s and early 80s.

T is for TEMIK, otherwise known as Aldicarb. A favorite among potato farmers, it is now showing up in well water in Aroostook and Penobscot counties. TEMIK is banned on Long Island because of its persistence in well water there. It is "temporarily" banned in Florida. Union Carbide sold 195,000 pounds of it to Mainers in 1981. A few drops of the concentrated liquid on the skin will kill the average man. Humans poisoned by as little as .1 milligrams of TEMIK for each kilogram of body weight suffer from nausea, muscular weakness and slurring of speech. "You eat a little bit of Temik every day. I guarantee it," says Dr. Robert Harris of Union Carbide. "Who's to say it doesn't make you feel better?"

T is also for 2,4,5-T (which isn't an unorganized township, although its name makes it sound like it should be); 2,4,5-T was outlawed in Maine in 1978, yet it still showed up in 1983 soil samples, persisting four years after its manufacturer, Dow Chemical Company, said it should. It is one of the ingredients in Agent Orange and contains Dioxin, "the most toxic chemical on earth." Director Robert Denny of the Board of Pesticides Control offers small consolation: "As long as people are not eating the soil, the persistence (of 2, 4, 5-T) will probably not pose a health hazard."

U is for UNWANTED, UNINVITED & UP-TO-THE-MINUTE. Insects invade Maine from all directions including from over the Atlantic. Many of them find Maine's climate and foodstuffs so agreeable they decide to settle here permanently. Ever to our rescue, the Maine Department of Agriculture has set up traps for these invaders on the outer islands of Matinicus and Vinalhaven. Not meant to stop the invasions, the traps do manage to catch a few bugs and give farmers a week or two warning before the deluge.

V is for VELPAR, the new miracle pesticide of the blueberry industry. Marketed with the expectation to increase blueberry yields by over fifty percent, Velpar may be responsible for a blueberry glut that will put all but the big growers and their banks out of business. Its manufacturer, DuPont, is slow in releasing lab results to the public.

W is for WATER. As an unwilling accomplice in pesticide sprays, water has let us down.

X is for BRAND-X. What do you mean you don't know the names of all the pesticides you swallowed today in your food?

Y is for aYUH. That's what you say when you learn you've been poisoned by pesticides.

1958 — The Good Old Days: A typical DDT fish kill.

"Immediately after the 1958 spruce budworm spraying," says a Department of Inland Fisheries and Game report, "moribund suckers were observed in large numbers in Big Goddard Brook. These fish exhibited the typical symptoms of DDT poisoning; they swam erratically, gasped at the surface, and exhibited tremors and spasms...Fish were often seen floating passively downstream in a weakened and moribund condition. In several instances, blind and dying trout were found floating passively downstream more than a week after spraying." Some 302,000 acres of the Maine woods near Presque Isle were sprayed with DDT that year.

Z is for ZERO. That's how much we know about the long-term effects of pesticide use. "Those responsible for deploying chemical agents in vast quantities today should be aware that they may be held responsible for the health and medical consequences discovered at a later time." (The Maine Association for Human Genetics.)

1979 — Modern Times: Dennysville

"We waved our hats and waved our arms. The helicopter kept coming and the spray kept coming down."

From June 28-30, the St. Regis Paper Co. sprayed the defoliants Tordon 101 and Esteron 99 on 360 acres of clear-cut land near Dennysville (pop. 296), an impoverished Washington County hamlet. Strong winds ("too windy to cast for salmon") ignored by St. Regis and the Northeast Helicopter Service also carried the defoliants into neighboring Pembroke, Edmunds, Perry and Robbinston. State investigators found so much contamination that the Board of Pesticides Control warned residents not to eat from their gardens.

"Nobody has the answers, nobody," said Dr. Frank Lawrence, Director of the Maine Poison Control Center, when asked about the long-term effects of the spraying. St. Regis eventually agreed to reimburse residents for the value of the damaged produce, if they agreed to release St. Regis from liability once the company paid them off. Most signed, but some sued St. Regis and Northeast Helicopter for $100 million. The case is still in the courts.

"It made my eyes burn, it made my lungs hurt when I breathed."

1983 — That'll Take Care of Him...

Bo Yerxa is one of Maine's famous antipesticide activists. As the *Maine Times* tells the story, in 1983 he paid $18,000 for a hundred-acre Aroostook County farm. Bo knew the farm, or at least thought he did (his father's farm is next door), so he didn't bother to inspect the house carefully before buying it. The first time he walked in the house as owner, he could smell he had a hazard on his hands. He went down to the cellar and found the soil caked with orange-colored pesticides. Several containers had rusted and leaked.

"It's not unusual to find pesticide containers around a farm in Aroostook County," said David Marshall of the Farmers Home Administration, the agency which sold Yerxa the house and presumably knew about the contamination, but didn't warn him. Yerxa tried moving the chemicals from the cellar to the shed, but the brief contact left him with "two days of seemingly simultaneous chills and sweating and the initiation of a flu/cold syndrome that lasted weeks."

A soil test showed 110,000 parts per million (ppm) contamination of Premerge in the first two or three inches of soil and 140,000 ppm in the six- to twelve-inch range. Premerge (also known as Dinoseb) is "at the top of the list of pesticides that have failed government retesting." It is on the Maine restricted-use list.

12 Endangered & Unendangered Species

Endangered Species

BALD EAGLE: officially listed as endangered by the federal government. New England's only nesting pairs are in Maine (74 as of 1983). Once there were at least a thousand in the Pine Tree State; logging, shooting, highway construction, environmental contamination, disturbance and destruction of nests, pollution-caused depletion of the food supply, poisoning, defeathering ("historically the sale of bald eagle feathers has been big business") and DDT ended that. Merrymeeting Bay used to be the Number One nesting ground in Maine; today the Cobscook Bay area holds that distinction (Merrymeeting boasting only two nests). UMO's Bald Eagle Project keeps count and responds to medical and other emergencies. In 1981 they built an "artificial" bald-eagle nest on an island off Mt. Desert in the same tree of a nest that had been blown down in 1979. In 1983, two eagles moved in and hatched an eaglet. When asked how Bernie Thompson of the UMO project knew how to fashion an artificial nest that the birds would like, Kent Wommack of the Nature Conservancy said Thompson "has been in almost every eagle nest in the state; he knew what they looked like."

BIRDS: Of Maine's 191 breeding species, the state's Critical Areas Program lists eighty-two (forty-two percent) as having "high priority for protection."

BOX TURTLE: "Threatened by excessive collecting."

BUTTERFLIES AND MOTHS: Critical Areas Program lists thirty-nine Maine species as rare. Some examples: *Katahdin Arctic:* only place in the world it is found is the Mount Katahdin plateau. *Early Hairstreak:* considered "the greatest prize of northern collectors"; recognized, therefore, by the pin through its gut. *Ommatostola:* has only been collected at Kittery. *Lygris:* only individual ever collected in Maine was on Mt. Bigelow in 1952; also distinguished by pin through gut. *Pipevine Swallowtail:* common in Southern states, but rare in Maine.

CANALS: Fifty years of intense nineteenth-century activity built 150 miles of canals in Maine. Railroads and shady financing did them in. *Songo Locks* between Long and Sebago Lakes is an example of one of the few remaining operable locks in Maine.

COAST, PUBLIC: Twenty-three percent of the coast nationwide is publicly owned; in Maine only four percent is public. Less than two percent of Maine's coast is beach, and of those precious seventy-seven miles, only a fifth is publicly owned. Less than that is accessible, however. No-parking signs at public beaches are common. Few beaches cater to the masses. Even where parking exists, landowners block ancient right-of-ways. Some beaches you can't drive to (Jewell Island, etc). Some are tainted; East End Beach in Portland was closed from 1955 to 1980 because of water pollution. A new city sewage plant supposedly makes it safe to swimmers again; 5,700 bathers were brave enough to test those waters in 1982.

CRITICAL AREAS PROGRAM: In 1983, federal funding for Maine's critical areas program was cut back. Located in the basement of the State Planning Office in Augusta, the Critical Areas Program, which keeps tabs on Maine's endangered species and threatened environments, has had its staff cut back to one and is itself endangered.

DEER: Maine's Number One game animal; numbers can fluctuate wildly. Declining numbers caused the state for the first time in 1983 to limit deer hunting to bucks only throughout much of the southern and eastern parts of the state. The beleagured deer has many enemies including hunters, heavy development, "people pressure," loggers, spruce budworm, coyotes, dogs, pesticides, starvation, cars, trains, and bright lights (at night, on the highways).

DUNES: Very rare in Maine. Popham Beach is the showcase example. They provide the only nesting habitat for rare birds such as the least tern and piping plover.

ESPERANTO: International language, invented in 1897 by Polish linguist Ludwig Zamenof for the "promotion of world peace through better communication"; spoken by fewer than ten Mainers. "For the past thirty-seven years, my family has vacationed in Maine," translates into Esperanto as "Por la pasinta tria deka sep jaraj mian familio restas en Maino." It's difficult to imagine Down Easters calling their homeland "Maino"; perhaps this is why the language has never caught on.

FOUR-TOED SALAMANDER: Only a handful of sightings in Maine of this black-spotted, white-bellied creature have been reported.

FUNGI: The most specialized of all may be *Geaster spp.* ("earth stars") only found at "the

FROM THE *UNCENSORED* NEWS SERVICE

> ### Maine deer looking forward to the year 1989
>
> **AUGUSTA** — Figures released from the Department of Inland Fisheries and Wildlife show that 23,794 deer were killed in Maine's 1983 "bucks only" season. This continues the downward trend in the number of deer killed in Maine in recent years.
>
> In 1980, 37,255 deer were killed. In 1981 the number was 32,035; 1982 it was 28,702.
>
> If the downward trend continues at its current pace, by the year 1989 no deer will be killed in Maine.

Desert of Wayne" (a wind-deposited inland dune, a rare formation in Maine; the more famous "Desert of Maine" in Freeport is another example of these short-lived natural features).

FURBISH LOUSEWORT: Maine's first officially listed Endangered Species. Grows nowhere else in world except upper St. John River Valley. Thought to be extinct until 1976 when found in proposed Dickey-Lincoln Dam flood area. Called "the little ugly plant that stopped a dam." It was "discovered" in 1880 by Brunswick's "nature nut" Kate Furbish in Van Buren. A 1983 Critical Areas Program survey estimated that the lousewort population at five thousand individuals, "occurring in 28 locations between T14 R13, Maine and Aroostook, New Brunswick." Lousewort reproduction "is entirely by sexual means."

GEESE: During June, 1983, over eight hundred Wild Canada geese were trapped on a Connecticut golf course and let loose in Maine. This transfer of "nuisance geese" from southern golf courses to Maine is becoming more common as the Maine Department of Fish and Wildlife attempts to restock the Maine scene.

GIRLIE SHOWS: Once standard fare at nearly all Maine fairs; in 1983 could only be found in Fryeburg thanks in large part to the Topsham girlie show scandal of 1981. (See page 65.)

GOLD: Very little in Maine. Best gold panning site is the Coos Canyon area of the Swift River in Byron (site of first U.S. gold strike), but don't expect overnight riches. It is estimated that a summer of persistent hand-panning at this site might not even yield as much as an ounce (welfare pays better).

GREAT BLUE HERON: Rookeries exist on some fifteen-plus coastal islands, such as Upper Goose Island (Harpswell), Wreck Island (Bristol) and Outer Heron Island (Boothbay); and inland at twenty-plus locations such as a small island in the Androscoggin River in Leeds and another island at the south end of Cobbosseecontee Lake in West Gardiner.

HIPPY HOMESTEADERS: First colonies reported in Maine in late sixties; no accurate population survey then or since has been done, but generally acknowledged to be declining. Few known nesting colonies remain, and the Critical Areas Program has yet to designate any as worthy of protection.

RECENT EXTINCTIONS

Caribou

Cullaloo

Eastern Elk

Giant Sea Mink

Passenger trains

Wolf

Wolverine

NOT IN MAINE

Whooping Crane

AIDS

Poisonous snakes

Dinosaur bones or tracks

Active volcanoes

LEAST TERN: Less than one hundred in Maine. Prefers to nest in a "broad, open, sandy beach with scattered pebbles and bits of shell." This is also the summertime preferred habitat of humans. The tern's fragile nesting sites (only three in Maine are known) are easily disturbed by beach development, off-road vehicles and innocent (or not-so-innocent) passers-by, not to mention storms, predators (gulls, crows, owls, sparrow hawks, foxes, skunks, racoons, ants, snakes, rats, etc.) and high tides. The first tern nesting site in Maine, discovered in 1961 in Scarborough, was eventually destroyed by a housing development. During 1981-82 Maine Audubon unsuccessfully tried to stop the construction of two houses near the tern nesting site at Goose Rocks Beach in Kennebunkport. The day after the initial hearing on the permit, "someone cut off the head of a porcupine and put it on a stick in the middle of the colony." That's another way to get rid of them.

LOON, COMMON: In 1982 Maine Audubon counted 388 adults and 97 chicks in 121 lakes. The loon's most noticeable disappearance has been in southern Maine where human use of the lakes has disturbed the loon habitat. Predators such as gulls and racoons, following in man's wake, have also contributed to the decline.

MARTENS: Wiped out on the Maine coast by overtrapping; still trapped inland; pelts sell for $20-25. Currently being restocked on coast by Fish & Wildlife biologists.

MONADNOCKS: Scarce. Monadnocks are hills of resistant rock on a peneplain. Mt. Agamenticus in York County is the point of intersection of three climatic zones and was no doubt sacred to the Indians. Today it is scarred by a road to the top (which destroyed the only known native stand of flowering dogwood in the 1940s), an abandoned ski resort and a microwave tower. "Great place to observe migrating hawks."

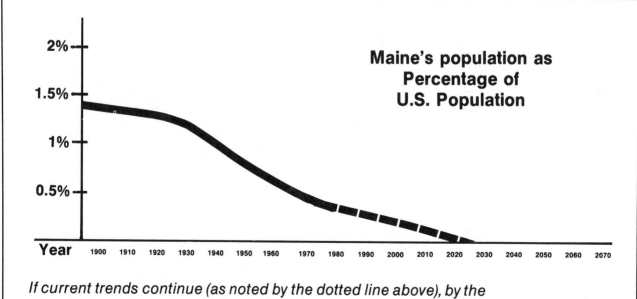

Maine's population as Percentage of U.S. Population

If current trends continue (as noted by the dotted line above), by the year 2027 no one will be living in Maine.

MOSS, LUMINOUS: Reflects green light in dark environments, such as caves, rock crevices, rabbit holes, cracks, shaded rock faces, under barns, uprooted trees and boulders. Only a handful of sites have been found in Maine; Bald Porcupine Island (Bar Harbor) is one.

NEON SIGNS: Not as spectacular as luminous moss, and declining. One of the last Holiday Inn neon signs anywhere is in Waterville.

OYSTERS: A herpes virus was found in American oysters in the Marsh and Piscataquis Rivers during 1970. According to Kenneth C. Young Jr., Deputy Commissioner of the Department of Marine Resources, this herpes virus cannot be transmitted to humans. But you know what they say about oysters. (Very few in Maine, though.)

QUICKSAND: A quicksand bog at Monson (Piscataquis County) and a quicksand pool on Deer Hill (Oxford County) have been documented.

SMALL WHORLED POGONIA: A member of the official U.S. endangered species list. Called the rarest orchid in North America. About half of the world's population is thought to occur in two isolated sites in Maine.

TURKEY, WILD: Ben Franklin's favorite bird. Between five hundred and three thousand thought to be in Maine, which, unlike Vermont, New Hampshire, Massachusetts, New York and Connecticut, does not have a spring turkey-hunting season.

VEGETARIAN RESTAURANTS: Nearly impossible to find in Maine in their pure form because it's difficult to make a profit serving brown rice and miso on tables too small to fit your legs under.

WOODSIA ALPINA: May become the Furbish Lousewort of the '80s. The largest population of this rare fern is found in an area on the banks of the Penobscot River that would be flooded by the "Big A" dam being proposed by the Great Northern Paper Co. Also rare in Vermont and New York, the only other two Eastern states where it is known to occur. (The Furbish Lousewort was the rare plant that helped kill the Dickey-Lincoln dam for the St. John River.)

YELLOW-NOSED VOLE: An alpine rodent with a yellow nose that has been found in only four locations in Maine, one of them being Sugarloaf mountain. Look for one on your next trip down the slopes.

*Un*endangered Species

BLACK FLIES: Maine State Insect. See map.

CARP: Otherwise known as garbage fish. Blamed for crowding out salmon and other "desirable" fish. Hated in Maine almost as much as the coyote.

CATS: No matter how many are destroyed by animal shelters there are always too many. During the summer of 1983, Searsport announced it was going to round up its estimated one hundred stray cats and get rid of them. Some phone callers protested and were irate. When asked what the callers said, Town Clerk Sue Lessard replied: "If I deleted the four-letter words, the conversations didn't [amount to] much."

COCKFIGHTS: Illegal, but widespread. Never in the same place twice.

COON CAT: Famous for littering the house with hair. Oftentimes mistaken for a rug.

CORMORANTS: Prey on salmon. Hated almost

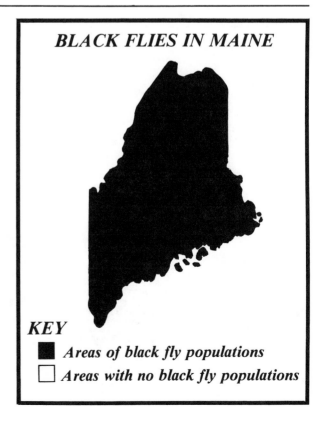

BLACK FLIES IN MAINE

KEY

■ *Areas of black fly populations*

□ *Areas with no black fly populations*

5 WAYS TO BEAT THE BLACK FLY...

As we stumble toward the year 2000, it is becoming increasingly clear that Maine's traditional methods of killing the black fly are outdated and inadequate.

The most popular method during the past two centuries was the industrial and civic pollution of Maine's rivers, streams and lakes. This method was partially successful in controlling the black fly population since the female will only lay her eggs in unpolluted water. During the past fifteen years, in a rush to clean up Maine's waters, our legislators have inadvertently helped to create an abundance of new black fly nesting grounds. If this zeal to do good continues, the black fly population is liable to explode and become truly unbearable.

Obviously, new methods of controlling the black fly are needed. Some suggestions:

1. *Relive the Good Old Days:* For ten thousand consecutive black-fly seasons, aboriginal Mainers coated their bodies with bear grease. This method was a big success then; there is no reason to think it won't work today.

2. *Make rain:* The black fly does not like to mate in a heavy rain. The governor could initiate a statewide cloud-seeding program. If this doesn't produce the desired "negative population" rainfall, then Wilhelm Reich's cloudbuster over to Rangeley should be unchained and pressed into use. (See page 58.)

3. *Go White:* Maine is already ninety-nine percent white; there's no reason why we can't go whole hog. Since the black fly is repelled by white clothing, white from head to toe could become the required Maine dress. We could also develop a religion to go along with this and call it Indoor Tennis.

4. *Make Wind:* The black fly hates a heavy wind. A gigantic nuclear wind generator could be built in Kittery and aimed toward the Maine woods. The heavy winds produced will discourage the black fly's social life. More likely than not, this method will completely drive the black fly from Maine, although our Canadian neighbors might not appreciate it.

5. *Lie Low:* One way to get relief from the vicious black fly is to lie on the ground. Remarkably, the black fly will think you are playing dead and stop bothering you. This horizontal position may become popular and be adopted as the new Maine posture. Lying on the ground with a member of the opposite sex might help reverse our declining birth rate.

Seagulls spontaneously generate at Maine dumps

as much as the coyote. Impossible to eradicate: "Massive egg-destruction projects at rookeries are quickly negated by renesting birds."

COYOTES: Newcomer to Maine since World War II. Hated for eating deer and sheep; blamed for everything else that goes wrong, too. Impossible to eradicate: they're too smart. Will probably invade Portland someday; they've already been spotted in Waterville.

CROWS (AND RAVENS): Roadkill keeps the population up.

DUNKIN' DONUTS: More popular than church on Sunday.

GASOLINE FUMES: Rats and mice exposed to them develop kidney cancers.

MARIJUANA: Weed; grows everywhere.

NO-SEE-UMS: Almost as widespread as the amoeba.

POACHING: Illegal, but widespread. Also known as "jacking."

POT HOLES: Route 11 between Patten and Fort Kent is the textbook case.

PUCKERBRUSH: Has yet to reach its economic potential. Doesn't win any popularity contests, either.

REAL-ESTATE AGENTS: It is rumored every adult Maine person is a real-estate agent.

RED TIDE: Like nuclear radiation it cannot be seen, smelled, heard, tasted or felt. "As little as 0.000035 ounce will paralyze the lungs of an adult in about two hours." Enjoy your mussels and clams.

RESTAURANTS CALLED "THE LOG CABIN"

SEAGULLS: Rats with wings.

SLUGS, WOODCHUCKS, RACOONS, ETC.: Found in gardens everywhere.

SWIMMERS' ITCH: "It's a parasite that's been around forever," so they say. Sebago Lake population is well established. Most noticeable beginning in August.

TOURISTS: Number One unendangered species. Hunted more than the deer. Scalps considered valuable.

Bangor Daily News

Artificial coyote being tuned up by Fisheries and Wildlife Department worker. These robots deceive real coyotes, then kill them with poisoned fangs. They have also been responsible, so it is alleged, for the death of seventeen Maine children. On the death of one family's three children, a Fisheries and Wildlife spokesman commented: "It is regrettable, but no price is too high to pay for the extermination of these predators of our deer herd."

THE MOOSE THAT ROARED

The Maine State Legislature passed a law in 1981 that made it legal for the first time in forty-six years to hunt and kill Maine's official state animal, the moose. When news of the vote reached the moose they could hardly believe their ears. They had gotten used to a peaceful coexistence with Mainers and didn't want to give it up. A pow-wow was called and a representative moose named George was elected to travel the treacherous route to Augusta to plead the cause of the moose.

The state legislators were unsympathetic. They said the forty-six years of peace had created too many moose and there wasn't enough food in the woods for them and soon many would die of starvation. A hunt was needed to thin out the moose and keep the race healthy and strong. George disagreed. He said paper company clear-cuts created the conditions for a plentiful supply of new woods growth, the moose's favorite food. Besides, his brother and sister moose preferred a natural death, even if it was starvation, to being hunted, a practice which would disrupt the moose's family and social structure. But the state legislators were unyielding and finally admitted they would never get re-elected if they listened to George's arguments. There was nothing he could do or say otherwise; he went back home.

When he told the rest of the moose what happened in Augusta some of them got angry. "How dare they declare war on us," proclaimed a fiesty young buck moose. "We must strike back now, before it is too late!" But calmer heads prevailed, as most moose elected to take a wait-and-see attitude.

In the fall of 1982, during the first "official" moose season (there had been an "experimental" season during 1980) about 1,000 moose were shot. The surviving moose were very upset to see their loved ones dragged away from them, especially before they had had a chance to finish mating. Morale in the land of the moose was low.

In 1983 about the same number of moose were once again destroyed. Another pow-wow was called. For three days and nights debate raged on. In one camp were the moose who urged their comrades to take up arms and fight back against the people of Maine. The other camp said Mainers were too heavily armed and fighting against them was contrary to the nonviolent moose tradition.

Finally, after all the other moose had exhausted themselves debating, they turned in desperation to George, pleading with him to speak up once and for all.

So George rose up and said: "We are a nonviolent animal. But these are unusual times. The choice today is not a choice between violence and nonviolence; it is between nonviolence and survival. We must survive. We must fight back!" And when George said this the other moose let out a mighty cheer, for he had united them and given them hope.

The moose formed an army and called themselves SMOOSARF, which stood for the *State of Maine's Only Official State Animal Revolutionary Front.* They smuggled Russian-made AK-47 rifles across the Canadian border and mounted them on their antlers. They made hand grenades out of pine cones, and

The One & Only!

BLUE-BACKED TROUT: Only found in ten headwater lakes of the St. John and Penobscot Rivers. "It was extirpated from the Rangeley Lakes around 1900."

DE SOTO, 1959: Auto registrations for 1981 show only one of these left in Maine, in Aroostook County.

HILTON: The Airport Hilton Inn (Bangor) is the only Hilton in Maine.

JOCKEY CAP (Fryeburg): Called the world's largest boulder by *NATIONAL GEOGRAPHIC.*

KATAHDIN MT.: Boasts over 30 plant species, 25 that occur nowhere else in Maine.

LITCHFIELDITE: An igneous rock, named for Litchfield, Maine, "the only locality in the world where it is known to occur."

MARINE SEDIMENTS, ANCIENT: Found at their highest elevation (305 feet) in Moscow (Somerset County).

MAZE: Largest manmade maze in Maine has been constructed in the Harpswell woods by artist David Brooks of the Acme Maze Company.

coyotes taught them guerilla-warfare tactics (such as how to move through the woods silently and not be seen).

On the first day of the 1984 moose-hunting season, the moose attacked Greenville (the center of the moose-hunt activity) at dawn. They shot and killed 179 very surprised hunters, who were easy marks in their bright orange outfits. The moose completely overran Greenville, firebombing and destroying houses, trucks, roads, bridges, cars, trains, official weigh-in stations and moose-meat refrigeration units. Their business done, they retreated to the hills, leaving the town in shambles.

Upon being notified of the attack, Governor Brennan acted quickly. He called the President. The President sent the Marines on a "rescue" mission to Greenville in order, as he put it on national TV, "to save Mainers from the moose."

After the Marines landed in Greenville, they followed the moose into the hills. The cold Maine weather was a stumbling block, however, as the Marines were used to fighting in the warm Carribean and Mediterranean climates. Many died of frostbite. Still, with their overwhelming firepower, they managed to beat the moose back toward Baxter State Park.

When moose got to the park's borders, they attacked the gates, killing all of the park rangers on duty. Establishing their own sentries at the gates, they then dug a moat with their hooves around the two-hundred-thousand-acre park, mined its borders with porcupines and withdrew to Mount Katahdin. When the Marines arrived in hot pursuit, many of them drowned in the swift-running moat or got pricked by the powerful mines.

The Marines regrouped, and the Joint Chiefs decided to attack the park by air. Things looked grim for the moose. Their only defense against air attack was a couple of rusty old anti-aircraft guns they had bought cheap at a lawn sale in Dover-Foxcroft and which they had positioned on top of Katahdin. The Marines, on the other hand, had hundreds of B-52 bombers and F-15 fighter planes.

But then the miracle the moose had been hoping for happened. Newspaper columnist and moose lover John N. Cole (who had led, the previous year, an unsuccessful referendum to outlaw the moose hunt) called the Joint Chiefs. He told them that Baxter State Park must remain forever in its wild state and that this was law. Bombing the park, Cole pointed out, would destroy much of the park's natural habitat and was thereby illegal.

The chiefs called up the President and asked him what to do. The President heard the chiefs out and said: "As much as I hate to say it, we must obey the law. Forget about the bombs, we have no choice but to negotiate."

The President sent Henry Kissinger to Maine. He had had experience negotiating many years before. The moose sent George to meet him.

"Checkmate," said George. "We can wait you out forever. We're used to the food. Already your Marines are becoming bored and restless with nothing to shoot at. Why don't you send them where they'll be useful and not such an eyesore on the landscape."

Kissinger had no choice but to agree. A peace treaty was signed. The surviving Marines were sent on a new mission, to Florida, to fight the manatee. And the moose were never hunted again.

OLD SOW WHIRLPOOL (Eastport): One of the largest (and most dangerous) whirlpools in the world thanks to average tides of eighteen or more feet.

RED FIN PICKEREL: "Possibly the rarest fish species in Maine." Only three individuals have ever been found (1977, in a Merrymeeting Bay tributary). So little is known of this fish that no one is even sure if it's a native.

SEBAGO: Deepest (315 feet) lake in New England.

STARLIKE SAXIFRAGE: Mount Katahdin is thought to be the only place in the lower forty-eight states where it grows. "Given the furor over collection in earlier times," says a state Critical Areas Program report, "it's almost surprising that this species still occurs on Katahdin." There are early accounts of

botanists picking every specimen they found. A 1901 account reveals the usual method: "To Williams is due the credit for finding her, and of tearing her ruthlessly from her damp bed under the dark rocks."

TREES, LARGEST: Maine towns boast the tallest examples in the entire U.S. of some species. For example — *Eastern White Pine* (Blanchard); *Pitch Pine* (Poland); *Tamarack* (Jay); *White Paper Birch* (Hartford).

UNION CHURCH, ALNA: World's smallest church; at publication time, had been taken apart.

ZOOS: Aqualand Animal Park (Bar Harbor) was named one of the ten worst zoos in the country in 1983 by the Humane Society. "We had a bad director, and he pulled the wool over our eyes."

DID YOU KNOW?
☐ DO YOU CARE?

...that the first cows to land in Maine came from Denmark?

...that Swan's Island off Mount Desert is the only island in Maine with an "official" apostrophe "s" in its name?

...that Charles Dickens once bought sponge cake in North Berwick?

...that one of Abraham Lincoln's pallbearers is buried in East Soneham?

...that the mausoleum in South Windham is sometimes mistaken for George Washington's tomb?

...that one of Sitting Bull's tomahawks is on display in East Limington?

...that casing for the neutron bomb was once manufactured in a Naples machine shop?

...that Rudy Vallee first learned how to wave a baton in Westbrook?

...that the return rate of spawning salmon from Maine's fish hatcheries is less than 1 percent?

...that the most popular place name in Maine is mud? There are 65 Mud Ponds, 14 Mud Lakes and 12 Mud Brooks.

...that Lincolnville used to be named Canaan and Canaan used to be named Wesserunsett; that Wellington used to be named Bridgetown and Monticello used to be named Wellington; that Pittsfield used to be named Warsaw and Poland used to be named Bakerstown; that Orrington used to be named China and China used to be named Harlem; that Smithfield used to be named East Pond and Litchfield used to be named Smithfield; that Newport used to be named Great East Pond and Blue Hill used to be named Newport; that both Garland and Thorndike used to be named Lincoln and Trenton used to be named Thorndike and Lincoln used to be named Mattanawcook; that Belgrade, Brooks, Mount Vernon and Newfield all used to be named Washington and Washington used to be named Putnam; and that both York and Gray used to be named Boston, and Clifton used to be named Maine?

...that the Belfast & Moosehead Lake Railroad has not yielded stock dividends for fifty-six years?

...that thirty percent of Maine people receive foodstamps?

...that seventy percent of all the snowshoes bought by the government during World War II were manufactured by the Snocraft Factory of Norway?

Mark Melnicove

SALE

SHOE2

13 *Religion*

People in Maine are divided into three religious groups, Catholics, conservative Protestants (locally known as "Christers") and all others. This latter group includes everything from Jews to Quakers to atheists; one cannot be sure how many there are.

The first two groups are large and have often come into conflict. The French and Indian war, for example, which saw Father Rale and a number of Indians killed at Norridgewock in 1724. But in the last century, when civilization had supposedly come to the wilderness, the battle broke out again. In Ellsworth a town meeting in June of 1854 resolved "that should the said [John]

Bapst [Jesuit priest and missionary] show himself again in Ellsworth, that we manifest to him our gratitude for his kindly interference with our public schools, and his effort to banish therefrom the Holy Bible, by procuring for him and trying on an entire suit of new clothes, such as can be found in the shop of any tailor, and that when thus apparelled, we present him with a free ticket to leave Ellsworth upon the first *rail road operation* that may go into effect." (*Ellsworth Herald, Oct. 20, 1854*).

This threat, from a democratic town meeting, was carried out on the night of October 14, 1854, when the priest was tarred and feathered and

---

SOCIAL REGISTER OF CHURCHES IN MAINE
(from top to bottom)

EPISCOPAL — Where the rich who want to be Catholic, but don't dare, go to church.

CONGREGATIONAL — Last redoubt of Puritanism, but since Cotton Mather the sermons have been getting duller.

UNITARIAN — Have turned their churches into movie theaters and halls for discussion groups about divorce.

CATHOLIC — The largest church in Maine, divided into French and Irish congregations. There has never been a French bishop even though the French greatly outnumber the Irish. It has a loyal attendance on Saturday night and at beano games.

METHODIST — Socially active. Highest percentage of bean suppers. Also buries a lot of Maineiacs. Sermons here are very dull.

BAPTIST — So many shades of this church that each small town has at least two, the hard-shelled, who don't believe in dancing and the Sunday papers, and the softshelled, who do. Right up there with the Catholics for inculcating guilt.

SEVENTH DAY ADVENTISTS — A church for lower-middle-class vegetarians. They run excellent hospitals and come to the door only once a year.

CHURCH OF THE LATTER-DAY SAINTS — "Mormons." Most aggressive proseletizers. Won't take no for an answer until you ask them about polygamy.

PENTACOSTALISTS — At the bottom of the religious totem pole. They speak in tongues, rant and stomp. Fun for an evening but not for a steady diet.

carried out of town on a rail. This was at the height of the Know Nothing crusade. These fine Americans were antiforeign and anti-Catholic and were urged on in local and national pulpits by the likes of Lyman Beecher, Harriet Beecher Stowe's father. Newspapers also stirred up the fire of hatred, and the worst in the state was this same *Ellsworth Herald*, which kept up its circulation with rabid nativist spoutings and antipapist cant. The paper later became the *Ellsworth American*, now owned and edited by the renowned J. Russell Wiggins, formerly editor of the *Washington Post*. There have not been any tarrings and featherings in Ellsworth in recent years.

There was a second outburst of anti-Catholic feeling in the 1920s with the rise of the northern branch of the Ku Klux Klan. This was a very serious and large group. The qualifications for membership sound almost like the application form for the Know Nothings — no foreign-born or Catholics need apply. The Klan was so powerful that in 1924 it elected its candidate for Governor (Owen Brewster) by a large majority.

One of the authors of this book was brought up a Christer and used to attend church five or six times a week. He was "saved" by an English evangelist who spent a week at the local gymnasium drumming into the heads of all the local sinners how rotten they were and what relief Christ would bring them. Being a Baptist, the epitome of the Maine fundamentalists, he got used to hearing six times a week that hell would be the reward of those souls who didn't come across. Of course, not wanting to be a "dead soul," all the young people and some of the elders in the church

TEMPLE OF BACCHUS

Tom Jones

Religious observance reached new heights in Wells in 1978 when "Bishop" Carlisle Estes and "Cardinal" Vincent Morino announced plans to open the Temple of Bacchus restaurant (dedicated to food, drink and dancing) in Wells' historic residential district along Route 1. Estes' contention that "Divine food, Heavenly music, Esthetic paintings and sculpture, Sacramental wines, Spiritual beverages, Inspired writings, Ethereal dancing...(are) created by man through the guidance and worship of God through Bacchus" was frowned upon by the conservative Wells zoning board.

The board cited a zoning ordinance which prohibits restaurants in the historic Route 1 district as they turned down the Temple of Bacchus application. Carlisle and Vincent's religious credentials were that they had paid fees to the California-based Universal Life Church to become bishop and cardinal. They had hoped their mail-order religious affiliations would allow them to get around the zoning ordinance since churches are allowed to have suppers in the residential area. Pictured above, in the heady days of 1978 when it seemed their divinely inspired scheme might soar, are Carlisle and Vincent with guard dog, Lance.

became "saved" and were dunked in the baptistry in back of the altar. He remembers being all wet and runny in his white clothing and how disappointed he was in the minister because he wore fisherman's long rubber waders.

There were and are frequent revivals in Maine. Nearly every evangelical church has one or two a year with added tent revivals in the summer. This follows a good American tradition. From reading about some of the earlier revivals one can believe that much of the excitement is sexual. As the preacher relates it in *The Grapes of Wrath*, church and sex have many things in common and church is a way of bringing people together socially. Tales of the minister running off with the organist are still common. The tension, too, of the high emotion — being promised a golden house on a street of alabaster as a reward for salvation or on the other hand an eternal burning in the fiery lake of hell — could call up some dynamic images to the young and impressionable mind. These churches have other appeals. One of them is undoubtedly that illiberal churches lay out a plan for life that seems to make it easy to decide what to do, starting with the ten commandments and going on to cover almost every aspect of life. In a world that is very uncertain, this can be both comforting and dull.

Sitting in church all the hours of Sunday school, morning worship, youth service, evening service, prayer meeting on Wednesday and Missions Club can be very dull indeed unless you have the fine neck of a girl- or boyfriend to look at while sitting on the hard pew. The claim has been made that ninety-five percent of millworkers think about sex most of the time. It can't be much different in the mills of God. After all, one must do something to deserve all that fire and brimstone.

Maine has had its share of religious oddities. The two most famous had the Holy Land as goal and both of them made use of ships.

The first pilgrimage to Palestine was by a group of 186 formerly hard-headed Yankee men, women and children from the Jonesport area. It was led by a down-and-out but charismatic preacher, George Joshua Adams, a rum-soaked former Mormon. The pilgrimage left Maine on the bark *Nellie Chapin* in 1866. He had promised a land of milk and honey but instead they found flies, fleas and typhus. A number of them died and another group was rescued from the sand and rocks of Jaffa by the steamer that happened to

BURN! BURN!
ROCK AND ROLL!
(to an appropriate rock beat)

By the Jeezly,
the Reverend Mr. Beesley*
has discovered what everyone wants to know:
just how all the hidden lyrics go.

Backwards and forwards
he makes the records spin;
Hell will be the reward
of listening to this sin!

If Queen says
smoke marijuana,
is that revealing something new?
Now that everybody's gonna?

Beesley is a guardian
of all that is right and wrong;
especially when it comes to music,
he wants to quash the song.

He wants rock out of school
in far Caribou;
prayers should take their place,
nothing else will quite do!

So the students learn
Beesley will tell them what to do:
Others say put the records in the fire to burn
and consider next time it might be you!

The Reverend Mr. Beesley of Caribou is convinced that rock and roll is the devil's work and he intends to do it in. He has condemned such groups as Queen which mention drugs in their lyrics. It is Beesley's contention that this music should not be played in public schools because it represents a religion which is banned, as his is. Others advocate the burning of the offending records, which some Maine churchgoers have done. These record-burnings have attracted considerable attention in the press.

be carrying Mark Twain on a tourist trip. Most of those who made it back to the United States did not have the courage to face their former neighbors, and they scattered across the country. According to a recent report, several of the solid buildings that the colonists built are still standing in what is now Israel and may be restored as a memorial to what might have been.

The second ill-fated flight to missionize the holy places and bring infamy to Maine was the voyage of the schooner *Coronet*, in 1911, captained by Frank Sanford, a former baseball player and the leader of the Holy Ghost and Us Society of Durham, Maine. The society had built a big temple of worship called Shiloh on a hill in this small rural town near Lewiston. It was able to make do financially because each of the converts had turned over all his or her worldly goods and property to the group. The ship did not carry enough of the proper food and water. Several of the clan died of scurvy. For this crime of omission Sanford spent several years in the federal prison

in Atlanta and the fellowship shrank considerably. but it still functions in Durham and a dozen other places and still seeks converts. Though the original building of Shiloh is much reduced in size now, weekly services are still held there and the ship *Coronet* still sails out of Gloucester and up the Maine coast each summer. Sanford is no longer captain, however.

Maine is undoubtedly overchurched. In the small town of Richmond, population 2,600, there are two Baptist, one Episcopal, a Catholic, a Methodist, two Russian Orthodox, and one Ukrainian Orthodox (serving the local Eastern European colony), an indeterminate Truth Tabernacle, a Nazarene, and a Seventh Day Adventist church. These latter two congregations show to some degree the trend away from liberal creeds to more conservative beliefs. The Nazarenes meet in what used to be the Congregationalist building and the SDA holds its services in the former Unitarian church. Both of these older, more intellectual churches run by ship builders and sea captains have died out, and blue- and white-collar workers have replaced them with evangelism.

The only thing needed to complete the swing in Richmond is a romp'em-stomp'em Holy Roller (Pentecostal) church where they speak in tongues and foretell the future for the Lord. One can be sure the only reason we have no snake-handling churches in Maine is because Maine is one of the two states in the union with no poisonous snakes — of the reptile kind, anyway.

Richmond church: not Russian, but it looks it

14 Maine Lingo-istics

HOW TO PRODUCE THE GREAT MAINE NOVEL

There have been a few attempts by Mainers such as Sarah Orne Jewett in the nineteenth century or Stephen King in the twentieth century to write significant novels, but the latter is too violent and superstitious and the former too placid and innocent for greatness. Perhaps if someone were to come along with a mixture of these two talents we might have the local equivalent of Faulkner.

It is said that all great American writers from Poe to Hemingway were drinkers if not drunks. The reason Maine has not had any great writers may be that Prohibition was more or less in effect since 1851 when Neal Dow got the Maine Law passed. Even today, if a writer wants a solitary soak at home on Sunday to pay off the doggerel of Saturday night, in many places he or she has to wait until Monday to get a bottle. Anyone knows that being sober for even one day is enough to put off great writing for the rest of the week. Also, even today, when most small towns have some sources of ales and liquors, the writers are bound up by feelings of sin, having heard years of preaching against demon rum by the Christian Civic Temperance League. And because of the state monopoly, Maine has some of the highest liquor prices in the nation. If one combines years of guilt, unavailability and the high prices, it is easy to see why Maine writers can't get a good book out.

If towns in Maine are ever to become as well known as Oxford, Mississippi, the state must do something about this situation. That something must be cognizant of the usual condition of poverty among most writers of the state. Surely, a free daily liquor ration for all Maine writers is what is called for.

Administering this largess would be no problem for the already underworked Maine Arts and Humanities Commission. They could identify the writers and send out chits to the approved that could be redeemed in liquor stores, beer halls and bars. Of course, this could not be for an unlimited amount — the equivalent of two bottles of vodka a day (we have to do something with those excess Aroostook potatoes) should be sufficient. Any writer who can't get destroyed on that amount should be writing temperance tracts anyway.

Maine life also is just too placidly bovine to cause enough stimulation for the right stuff of great writing to be produced. Something should be done to make it *hot* for writers. This could range from mugging a potential novelist at the Acton Fair to introducing writers to beautiful members of the opposite sex (or the same sex, according to preference). Anything to keep them off balance. The beautiful people should come

---

It's "Mount Dessert," Not "Mount Desert"

In spite of the way it is spelled, Mount Desert Island is properly pronounced "Mount Dessert," and there is a fancy reason for it — not what out-of-staters probably think, that Maine natives can't even pronounce a simple word correctly.

Samuel de Champlain, the French explorer, when he first saw the bare, rocky hills rising from the Gulf of Maine, named them *L'Isle des Monts Deserts*, "Island of the Bare Hills," and the French pronunciation has persisted. So there.

Academie du Maine

The special language or lingo of Maine is one of its most precious assets. It is fast being lost because of the homogenizing effects of radio and television. We must stop this rapid mixing. We propose an academy like the Academie Francaise to retain the purity of the Maine language.

To judge the extent of the problem, we need only to look at one word — *Maineiac*. One of the authors was himself a Maineiac — he never heard the word Mainer. Now, after an author used the word Maineiac in an article in the *Maine Times*, a reader wrote in and strongly demanded that the word be stricken from the *Maine Times* stylebook. In *Maine Lingo*, John Gould uses Mainer in preference to Maineiac because of spelling problems. Surely some board of judicious language arbiters should decide when one or the other or both words are accurate and make a statement that all will abide by.

The French Academy has forty members chosen from the best of the writing and academic fields. The only woman member, incidentally, Marguerite Yourcenar, happens to be a resident of Northeast Harbor. She could give us advice on setting it up. We would not need the full forty people since Maine is smaller than France and a few of the English words we use are standard for the whole country.

The work of the board would be to arbitrate new words and decide on proper usages. It could also study neglected lingo-istic areas: Dictionaries could be compiled for the lumbering, quarrying, fishing, farming and millwork trades. For example, one might be curious to know what is the function of the four-foot-beam-dinker, the operator of which is frequently advertised for in the help-wanted ads of the *Lewiston Evening Journal*.

Think of some of the issues this body could decide: whether to abolish television in the state, the authenticity of humorist Tim Sample, the teaching of Maine lingo in the schools, proper pronunciation for out-of-staters.

There would have to be a very careful selection of people for the Academy. Maine natives will have to be chosen along with scholars who have made a study of the state. John Gould, though not a native, should be president, having devoted a lifetime to writing about Maine and the quirks of both the language and the people. There is no shortage of other likely nominees.

Keeping up standards would be hard work. A salary should be paid to the academicians. A bond issue to build an academy building would have to be approved, and the Legislature would have to appropriate a sum for travel. But this would be recouped by the increase in tourist traffic — for people would come to Maine not only to see its natural resources but to hear them.

from Rent-a-Muse in New York City. Muggers come from the same place. Since we don't have the great racial conflict that fueled so many Southern writers, both black and white, the Arts and Humanities Commission would have to foster programs exciting or at least explaining the bias against the Franco-Americans of Lewiston and the Finns of Knox County.

More could be done: a cape on the shore for summer stimulation and an apartment in a three-decker in Auburn or Westbrook for the winter. Transportation must not be overlooked. An old but working Volvo station wagon should be provided. For historical novelists, a team of horses and a buggy. Of course, the writer will not have time to care for the horses, so servants must be provided. One to care for the horses or the Volvo, a cook and a scullion, a butler to fend off drop-ins, and a maid for the Rent-a-Muse.

Now we are getting somewhere. A fifth of Popov (Maine's own vodka) is only $4.45 — two would be $8.90 a day or $3,148.50 a year. Say a mugging every three months at $485 per mugging, that would amount to $1,540 per year. Rent-A-Muse is expensive, because they only use the most beautiful and witty of people — say $16,000 for three months per year. A cape on the shore would be a minimum of $80,000, and rent for the apartment about $300 a month for six months or $1,800. A Volvo, ten years old — $2,500; gas, oil and repairs $5,000...well, it does add up. We calculate that after the initial investment of just over $200,000, the state could probably get away with $150,000 per year per writer — less than a bank president gets. Not bad for all the great literature that should be seen.

A Maine Sampler

KINKY AS A RAT IN A BARN — Refers to a term of sexual excitement — probably was originally "Frisky as..." When a rat is in a barn he is likely to find both the food and action in the hayloft. His only worry is the barn cat.

GURRY — The fine fish sauce with which any seafood may be improved. Available from lobstermen at a surprisingly reasonable charge.

AYUH — A common Maine endearment meaning: "I want to kiss you."

FRIGGIN' — Ayuh, you guessed its meaning, although even school teachers use it in class, it is so permitted in Maine.

BEAN BOOT — A specially-designed boot with a built-in pouch for carrying beans. The sweat from the foot cooks the beans and makes them tasty and tender for the campsite supper.

BIGGEST BUCKS IN MAINE CLUB — This refers to a measurement of the members. Often they wear a patch on their jacket to announce their exalted status to females.

GULL SENSE AND HAWK FEVER — Refers to the fact that a gull will go to the dump for dinner if there are no fish around, whereas a fish hawk will stay on the water and starve to death if there are no fish. Mainers are famous for their gull sense.

THOMASTON UNIVERSITY — Not the largest branch of the state university, but with the most dedicated student body, some of whom spend their whole lives working on further education.

SPECIAL FISHERMEN'S LINGO-ISTICS

FISHING IN THE GRASSGROUND — A method of land lobstering whereby the trap is set on the bank and the bait used is so strong that it attracts lobsters out of the water and into the traps.

SHEEP IN BOOTS — Anything old enough for sexual intercourse.

DRAGGER — A Maine transvestite.

CHEESE RIND — The first sign of plug rot.

WET SMACK — Lobsterman's version of a kiss.

CRAB TRAP — Fisherman's vernacular for a prostitute.

DEPTH FINDER — Playboy.

BUTT BLOCK — Constipation.

BILGE PUMP — Diarrhea.

PLUG ROT — Term for venereal disease.

Sarah & Stephen

Although there have been a medium number of medium-successful writers about Maine, such as Ruth Moore, John Gould and Kenneth Roberts, Maine has produced two very successful novelists, Sarah Orne Jewett and the miasmist Stephen King. The major work of the former, *The Country of the Pointed Firs*, a pleasant and gentle summer tale, shows the good side of coastal Maine in the late nineteenth century. Its success had the effect of insuring the predominance ever since of the bean-pot and lobster-pot school of writing in Maine in which everything is quaint and very little conflict arises except in the natural elements.

That this is only part of the story is evidenced by the court records of the same time now housed in the Maine State Archives. Jewett based her book on an area of Martinsville, a village in St. George, where she lived for a summer. The court records of Knox County, wherein St. George lies, show that there were many drinking, whoring and gambling institutions in the nearby town of Rockland. Throughout the county there were divorces based on beatings and desertion. Some of her acquaintences of the summer were wife beaters, child molesters and secret tipplers. Her pleasant picture was basically the same a two-week tourist might see today traveling the coast; it cannot be considered great literature.

Stephen King is currently one of the world's best-selling authors. He has, in some of his novels, put parts of Maine on the map, though they may be disguised slightly. This master of horror, who resides in Bangor, is not for the squeamish or those who desire to be uplifted by the literature they read. No one will confuse him with Tolstoy or even Harold Robbins. King started his career with a story describing the strangling or cutting of college coeds on foggy campus nights. He has since progressed through a grisly range of subjects until now he writes of a car that kills of its own volition. This fits his style, which tends to run over the reader.

Mark Melnicove

Raw material for Stephen King

Mark Melnicove

Typical guardhouse at a summer person's estate? No, it's a submarine lookout tower used during World War II on Bailey Island

15 *Architecture*

The Neglected Outhouse

Mark Melnicove

There is a dispute among the Maine cognoscenti as to what constitutes the worst architecture in the state. Opinion is about evenly divided between the Wedding Cake House in Kennebunkport, probably Maine's most photographed error, and the new Portland Museum of Art — imposed on us by wealth and some out-of-state architect. However, we won't dwell on the bad, but concentrate on the best.

One of the most important and fertile fields of Maine architectural study — and totally neglected — is the so-called out building. In the Southern states, the separate kitchens and smokehouses are considered almost equal in reconstructions to the main houses. But in the North, out buildings have been allowed to fall into disuse and decay. Think of these: henpens, turkey houses, horsebarns, carriage houses, rabbit pens, foxfarms, smokehouses, milksheds, well houses, tree houses and, of course, the essentials called plain outhouse, backhouse, privy or Old Tilley. The description of these buildings is soon to be lost altogether because of human neglect, but in our just-passed rural and even small-town life they were critical. The feeding and unloading of the American bowel much depended on the appendages to the main house. Surely they are worthy of deep study.

One can go to our State Historic Preservation Commission and ask for details on Carpenter Gothic houses or old train stations and find a wealth of information. But if you ask about Old Tilley, you will shuffle forth disheartened. This surely must be rectified before all the old darlings are gone in the onslaught of Thomas Crapper, Clivus Multrum and the gas toilet.

Now is the time to have the commission take

Tom Jones

Poor people's dwelling in Aroostook County. It is, however, very energy-efficient

the heights, depths and breadths, to take oral and aural histories, to try to bottle the sweet elixir of what has gone before. Photographs, measurements, and in-depth interviews with builders and users can still be done — not all life has been snuffed out of these yet. It would be assinine to ignore the wealth of colorful tales and tributes that these small generic buildings have engendered. Now is the time to strike and strike while the seat is still warm.

Colonial and Victorian houses have been studied to death, but when was the last time you saw a volume on the outhouse? There could be studies of in-house, in-barn, out-back and in-the-woods outhouses. Other studies could be done on the need for the one-, two- and three-holer, the effect of outhouses on the fortunes of the Sears Roebuck Company, the psychological damage in those who were chosen for the shovel-out. Surely, the wealth of material would be almost endless.

So, friends of rural arcana, write your legislator, call the commission and urge them to consider that among the lowly are the best that America has had to offer in the way of sound and necessary buildings. Tell them that it must not be neglected or we will end up with a gaping hole in the knowledge of American rural life.

Guy Gannett Newspapers

Ugliest building in Maine: Portland Museum of Art. Notice the falsity of the front

Maine mobile home

Mark Melnicove

Guy Gannett Newspapers

   This is trainer Frank Hileman with Trina, one of two dogs at the Brunswick Naval Air Station that live in the celebrated $46,000 doghouse, built with taxpayer money, seen in the background. Being "in the doghouse" has now taken on a positive meaning in Maine, where the human housing is typically far less costly or luxurious. A number of poorer natives in the Brunswick area have expressed an interest in moving in with the dogs, despite their reputation for fierceness.

Stephen B. Nichols

Westbrook College's Tomb of Modern Art

Mark Melnicove

Park in the center of downtown Augusta

In 1983 the *Uncensored Guide to Maine* ran a contest, advertised in the newspapers and television, for people to send in pictures and descriptions of "The Worst Place in Maine."

We got entries such as Knox County, the Thomaston cement plant, "studying for an English exam at the University of Maine at Fort Kent on the first day of bird-hunting season," and the restaurant and gift shoppe at the tip of Bailey Island. Many people seemed to feel that something that spoiled their view constituted the worst place in Maine.

However, the authors had no hesitation in choosing this postcard as the winning entry:

The Worst Place In Maine

```
"The Worst Place in Maine"

The inner bowels of a mill, specifically
Guilford Industries, any day, any season
rates the distinction as the worst place
in Maine.

The mill stench clings to worker's bodies
and the chemically treated cloth causes body
rash on may employees. The worker is totally
consumed by the mill which demands total
allegiance. Unknowingly his soul and life
is sold to the mill  --  How Sad!!

                    Sign me,

                    One Who Knows
```

We hasten to point out that we have no idea if Guilford Industries in Dexter is the worst mill, let alone the worst place, in Maine. So we are awarding the prize to "the inner bowels of a mill."

We are sure, in a state where job-related illnesses and injuries are forty percent higher than in the United States as a whole, many millworkers would agree with our choice. Anybody who is familiar with the state would, it seems to us, have a hard time disagreeing.

Yet, undoubtedly there will be people who will feel that if we criticize our industrial plants — even their inner bowels — at the merest insult, such as the publication of this postcard, they will move out of state, throwing thousands out of work, and many children will starve.

Well, we've published this to call the bluff of the you-say-anything-bad-about-us-and-we'll-move-out-of-the-state-crowd. If one single large industry moves out of state because of the publication of this postcard, we'll admit we were wrong! Watch and see.